THE STORY OF AMERICA IN PICTURES

THE STORY OF
AMERICA
IN PICTURES

ARRANGED BY ALAN C. COLLINS

INTRODUCTION BY CLAUDE G. BOWERS

DOUBLEDAY, DORAN & COMPANY, INC.

NEW YORK   1944

AUTHOR'S NOTE

★

ALTHOUGH an effort has been made to secure pictures for this book that would portray faithfully each event, the author realizes that many famous historical paintings were conceived without accurate knowledge of the facts, and that in the execution of some the artists intentionally romanticized scenes and people. Therefore, it cannot be said that every illustration herein is accurate.

The Outline which appears in the front of the volume should be referred to frequently in reading *The Story of America in Pictures.* In it the period of our history has been marked off into twelve "eras." In order to avoid confusion, it was thought wise to subdivide, character of the subject being the determining factor, the events taking place within the time-period of each of these major divisions. Although making for historical unity, such a plan rendered impractical a strictly chronological order throughout.

The author wishes to thank D. Jay Culver of New York for his help in collecting many of the illustrations for the years prior to 1900, and St. George L. Sioussat, former Professor of History at the University of Pennsylvania, for reading the text matter of the first four hundred pages of this book.

He further wishes to take this means of thanking all those who have, through the years, taught him or gave him the opportunity of learning most of what he knows and likes about writing, writers, and publishing—his father, the late Philip S. Collins, Vice-President and Treasurer of the Curtis Publishing Co., William Taeusch and the late George B. Dutton, when Professors of English at Williams College, the late Professor Irving T. Babbitt of Harvard University, Bob MacAllen and Tommy Hargis, when in the city room of the now-defunct *Evening Public Ledger* in Philadelphia, Barton W. Currie as Editor of *The Ladies' Home Journal,* C. Raymond Everitt, now Executive Vice-President of Little, Brown & Co., Curtis Brown of the London office, and Nellie Sukerman of the New York office of Curtis Brown, Ltd., Benjamin H. Stern, New York lawyer, and the late Major Eric Knight, author of *The Flying Yorkshireman* and of *This Above All.*

A. C. C.

Rydal, Pennsylvania

June 1935, and March 1944

OUTLINE

★

III. *The Revolutionary Period, 1767–1793.*

IV. *Consolidating the Country, 1789–1861.*

VIII. *Period of the War, 1914–1919.*

IX. *Post-War to Stock Market Crash, 1919–1929.*

X. *Market Crash to Pearl Harbor.*

XI. *World War II.*

XII. *The Presidents of the United States.*

INTRODUCTION

★

THE MOST FASCINATING HISTORY is pictorial, even though the pictures are in words. In his *French Revolution*, Carlyle has given us a magnificent gallery of paintings, and his book consequently is immortal.

The story of the past can be made deadly dull unless so told as to make the visualization of the scene possible. Because so many histories do not call forth pictures, history has been given a bad name among the masses to whom history is important.

Woodrow Wilson was convinced that the highest art in the historian is in the painting of the contemporary scene in the very atmosphere of the times. He believed in pictures. A distinguished friend and associate of the War President has collected all the moving pictures covering his career, and, by running them in their order of precedence, has preserved for the historians of posterity a more vivid and human record than can possibly be put in words.

It is easy to forget the details of what one reads; one never forgets the details of what one sees. Many years ago a few friends met in the bar of the old St. Charles hotel in New Orleans. Included in the party was Sergeant S. Prentiss, the most brilliant orator America has produced. The conversation turned to a lecture on art, being given that night by a famous critic to raise money for an art museum. Prentiss and one of the party preceded the others to the theater. As the others approached the meeting, a little later, they were amazed to hear roars of applause. The critic was not an orator. As they entered the theater they found the explanation—Prentiss was speaking. Summoned to the stage without notice, he had plunged with all his eloquence into an oration on the masterpieces of art, which, in mangled form, is happily preserved today. Not an artist, not a student of art, he had nevertheless been able on a moment's notice to speak on art with a brilliancy that few, if any, of his contemporaries could have approached. And the reason was that during a vacation a little before he had amused himself by turning the pages of a great portfolio of the artistic masterpieces of the world. He put the pictures he had seen in words. He felt the pictures as no reading of a text-book could have made him feel them.

By the same token the ideal way to study history is to journey to the scenes associated with mighty events after having read the story of what had occurred there. The layman may read and reread the descriptions of the battle of Gettysburg and remain in utter ignorance of the movements of the troops; but no man can visit the battlefield with its monuments, today, without being able to call before him the dramatic scenes in the clashing of the blue and gray. That which the eye sees is most deeply imprinted on the mind.

In this volume the compiler has sought, at great pains, to collect the pictures that most vividly tell the story of the United States from the beginning almost to the present hour. It is a panoramic history that is rich in inspiration. It serves a patriotic purpose in bringing before us each step of our development, and impressing upon us, as words can scarcely do, the Homeric achievements of our people. No written chronicle of England from the Boer War to the present can make the emotional appeal to be found in "Cavalcade." In the picture one can recapture the very emotions of the times.

And no nation lends itself more perfectly to the pictorial history than our own. Our progress has been all drama, and much can be told in pictures. Few nations have been more colorful in their story. Within the space of a few centuries we have seen a vast continent redeemed from the wilderness, and our people marching with giant and gallant stride to their place in the sun. This has been due to the youthful vigor and romantic daring of our race. Our story is a picturesque drama with innumerable scenes. The drama is here presented in pictures.

Here we have the discoverers giving a new continent to civilization, battling against savage natives and more savage nature, penetrating the wilderness, pushing through primeval forests, floating down unknown streams, planting blockhouses as the outposts of a new day. That is drama at its highest.

And then we see the pioneers settling in the wilderness, living in log huts, felling the forests, draining the swamps, bridging the streams, building the highways, cultivating the fields, erecting schoolhouses and churches—and that is drama too.

And then the pictorial drama of the Revolution—Patrick Henry in fiery action, Jefferson in the preparation of the Declaration, Washington and his ragged continentals, and in the camp that dismal winter at Valley Forge. And then that dramatic, colorful scene at Yorktown. The whole drama of the Revolution can be told in pictures.

The flag unfurled—and the flag moves on toward the far Pacific. Louisiana's destiny is joined with ours, an event as rich in color as any we have ever known. And, in the meanwhile, the pioneers of the tribe of Daniel Boone are building their cabins in the woods and guarding them with their long rifles.

And then the genius of Jefferson launches our first scientific expedition on the waters of the far West when Lewis and Clark, with a few audacious and hardy hunters and fighters, tramp the virgin wilderness or float in canoes on the swift and dangerous streams, and break a path for civilization through the forests and across the mountains to the western sea, battling against disease and hunger. What a picture!

The War of 1812? It can be recorded in three pictures—Washington in flames, Perry on Lake Erie, and Andrew Jackson behind the cotton bales in New Orleans.

The flag moves on, fluttering among the wild passes of Mexico as our brave soldiers charge their bloody way to victory—and California is ours!

And soon the discovery of gold in the new possession, and that can be told in pictures—the wild rush of rough enterprising men in search of fortune, the opening of mines, the army with picks, the wild scenes in the camps.

And then, the opening of the western lands to settlement, and the picturesque procession of the covered wagons, men, women, children, and dogs, over trackless miles—laughter and tragedy, smiles and tears; and finally the garden spot of America blossoms. What drama! What a picture!

Then comes the War between the States, and, for the first time on a large scale, photography takes up the work of the historian, and through the illustrated weeklies the folks at home can visualize the immortal struggle—the clash of armies, the scenes about the camps, the swinging march of soldiers along the dusty highways—Gettysburg, Missionary Ridge, the battles of the Wilderness. These pictures, happily preserved, tell the tale of superhuman courage and sacrifice.

And other wars—Dewey at Manila Bay, the battle of Santiago Harbor, the passionate charges on San Juan Hill; and then the World War, when, rising to unprecedented heights of idealism, two million youths in a crusading spirit sailed across the sea to perform miracles of building and fighting and to end the dreadful struggle of humanity. But

> "*Peace hath higher tests of manhood*
> *Than battle ever knew.*"

And the story of the United States confined to battles fought with sword and gun is a story scarcely told. The peculiar splendor of our national development with such unprecedented rapidity lies in our victories over material forces—in the creation of our industrial life.

This, too, can be told in pictures. The building of the railroads is all romantic drama, with heroes and villains—tremendous in the dreams of the builders, in the labor of the workers, in the audacity of the conceivers—a story as picturesque and thrilling as any in all the tide of time. And this drama of the building is preserved in pictures.

Not always admirable were the methods of the amazing figures who pioneered our industrial and financial life. There was, too often, the savage, selfish spirit of the ruthless individualist, who, convinced of the ultimate gain for all, brushed all ethics aside to press on with brutal force to the achievement. Happily the story of this industrial growth and financial development, as told in pictures, presents only the more inspiring side. There are few exceptions—the marching of Coxey's army, the picture of "Black Friday."

The whole of our history cannot be told in pictures, but through them we get the highlights; and when they cover the whole of our story from the discovery to the present we may in the course of an evening visualize and catch the spirit of the nation's onward march. Nothing could be more useful or desirable now when the cynic and the scoffer are so blatant in the land. "New occasions teach new duties," and changes inevitably must come to meet changed conditions. But each succeeding generation has rendered heroic service, stumbling and blundering as all human creatures must, but always moving forward. Here we have presented to the eye a remarkable collection of pictures through which our inspiring history marches in parade. They bring us nearer to the past, on which the present rests; they inspire us with a greater reverence for the dead generations that have fought and wrought magnificently for us, and they revive within us something of the old dreams and ideals.

CLAUDE G. BOWERS

INDIANS OF THE FOREST

There is no present unanimity of opinion as to the origin of the people found in North America by the early explorers. Scholars agree that at one time northwestern America and northeastern Asia belonged to the same cultural area, but whether the Indians came from Asia or the Asiatics from America is not established. For purposes of rough classification the Indians here when Columbus arrived divide into three groups, Indians of the forest, Indians of the plains, and Indians of the west and southwest.

INDIANS OF THE PLAINS

The various tribes of the forest differed but they had much in common because their mode of life was the same. The men hunted, mostly deer, and made war. Some fishing was done and the women made attempts at agriculture. They traveled on foot and in canoe, but the forest was their home, supplying them with virtually all their worldly wants. Vastly different were the many tribes of the interior who inhabited the great plains swarming with buffalo. They likewise lived by hunting, but agriculture played a somewhat more important part in their lives. It was not until they caught and tamed the progeny of the horses that had escaped from the Spanish conquerors that they secured mounts for hunting and warfare.

INDIANS OF THE WEST

The tribes of the southwest were mostly Pueblos. They lived in permanent houses, often many stories high, in which each room was the home of a family. They had developed agriculture to a high degree, possessed some domesticated animals, and had mastered the science of irrigation. There were tribes of a different sort in California, while to the south dwelt the Aztecs, and beyond them was the vanished culture of the Mayas. Despite his savagery, the Indian was possessed of much dignity and simple wisdom, bred in him by the vast areas of virgin land which were his home and his heritage.

LEIF ERICSSON DISCOVERS VINLAND

Many scholars claim that the hardy Viking, Leif Ericsson, discovered America. Son of Eric the Red who colonized Greenland, Leif, in about the year 1000, landed on a coast which he called Vinland, for some of his men had seen wild grapes growing. This was prob- ably either Nova Scotia or the New England of later times. Such was the shadowy prologue. It was to be almost five hundred years before the real drama of American history began.

COLUMBUS AND QUEEN ISABELLA

As the 15th century drew to a close, the world was ready for the real discovery of America. Some people were saying that the world was round and had asserted that it might be possible to reach the riches of the east by sailing west. It was assumed that the same ocean washed the coasts of China and Europe. The increasing restlessness found its "man of the hour", in Christopher Columbus. He had unshakeable faith in an idea and was willing to risk his life for it. He said he would reach the Orient by sailing into the Atlantic. For ten years he haunted the courts of Europe seeking a financial backer. At length the necessary money was borrowed on security offered by the Queen of Spain. That she offered her jewels for the purpose may be only a legend.

FROM THE PAINTING BY VACSLAV VON BROZIK.   COURTESY ART EDUCATION PRESS, INC., NEW YORK.

19

FROM THE PAINTING BY CHRISTIAN RUBEN.

THE VOYAGE OF COLUMBUS

Orders were issued to outfit Columbus with three tiny ships and, after great difficulties in securing crews, he set sail from Palos on August 3, 1492. A stop was made at the Canary Islands. Columbus kept two log books, one for himself and one to show his doubting crew. In early October the men began to grumble openly; some suggested throwing Columbus overboard. But the faith of the commander prevailed.

20

THE LANDING

On the evening of October 11th lights were seen, and the next day Columbus stepped ashore in the new world on a small island in the Bahamas, probably that which is now known as Watling's. The natives told him, by signs, of a country to the south. Toward it he sailed and found Cuba, but he was convinced that he had found the mainland of India. He then skirted Haiti, left half his men to plant a colony, and returned to Europe.

FROM THE PAINTING BY JOHN VANDERLYN.

21

THE CABOTS LEAVING LABRADOR

England's early claims to America had little to do with any exploration by her own citizens. John Cabot, born in Genoa and a citizen of Venice, induced Henry VII to outfit an expedition. In 1497 and 1498 Cabot, probably accompanied by his son Sebastian, explored the coast from Newfoundland to South Carolina. But England forgot the work of the Cabots until a century later, when she was only too anxious to recall their discoveries.

VASCO DA GAMA IN KALIKUT

A Portuguese navigator succeeded where Columbus had failed. In 1497
da Gama set out to discover the mysterious empire to the east. Heading
into the south Atlantic, and then turning east, he sighted the African coast
near the Cape of Good Hope, in the discovery of which he had however been
anticipated by Diaz. Rounding that "land's end" he continued east and
so, at last, was found the water route to India. He claimed the country and
returned home in triumph. The picture was made in 1747.

23

PRINTING VESPUCCI'S BOOK

Amerigo Vespucci survives in history because from him derive the names of two continents. He accompanied an expedition to South America in 1499. Years later there was published his account of the trip, in which he told of the wondrous sights he had seen, giving the impression that he was in command of the vessel and that its voyage antedated the third made by Columbus. Waldseemüller, a geographer, having Vespucci's account, and not that of Columbus, accepted the former's story and in 1507 called the new continent America, after the author's first name.

THE FOUNTAIN OF YOUTH

To the Spaniards in the West Indies the natives brought tales of a great land in which there was a spring having the power to confer perpetual youth. In 1513 Ponce de Leon set out to find the magic waters, and discovered the mainland near St. Augustine. He named the country Florida, sailed down the east coast of the peninsula, and part way up the west, and returned through the previously unknown Bahama Channel, a protected strip of water which was later to be the haunt of pirates.

CLAIMING THE PACIFIC

Balboa fled from his home in San Domingo pursued by debt, and seized the rule of a struggling colony in Darien. From there he journeyed overland to prove the truth of Indian reports of a vast ocean to the west. Coming to a ridge, he made his companions remain be-hind and, reaching the summit, first discovered the mighty Pacific. When he had made the long journey to the shore he plunged into the water, claiming on September 29, 1513, all the ocean in the name of the King of Spain.

MAGELLAN SAILS AROUND THE WORLD

Magellan, an expatriated Portuguese, whose expedition was the first to circle the earth, sailed from Spain in 1519. He discovered the tortuous passage around the tip of South America and eventually came out on the waters first seen by Balboa. He named the ocean Pacific be-cause of its gentle breezes. Reaching the Philippines after suffering great hardships he died. Sebastian del Cano continued the voyage, eventually bringing to Spain the great news that at last the east had been reached by sailing west.

FROM THE PAINTING BY CHAPPEL. CULVER SERVICE.

CORTEZ CAPTURES MEXICO CITY

Hernando Cortez left Cuba in 1519 to conquer Mexico. Reaching the main-land his boats became worm-eaten and sank. (Some say he burned them purposely.) At any rate, with his escape cut off, it was a question of win or perish. Fighting his way to the capital he captured Montezuma, butchered the natives, and helped himself to a vast wealth of gold and silver. His brilliant campaigns made many at home jealous and he was forced to return to Spain. He made another voyage, and on returning from it was received coldly by the king. Perhaps there was truth in his bitter taunt that he had given his sovereign more provinces than his ancestors had be-queathed him cities.

DISCOVERY OF THE MISSISSIPPI

One of the victims of the reputed wealth of "the Floridas" was Hernando de Soto who had had his appetite for gold whetted by the fortune he had acquired accompanying Pizarro to Peru. He sold part of his property, outfitted an expedition, and landed in Florida in 1539. The next four years he spent marching through the Southern states, ever seeking for gold, until in 1541 he came to the Mississippi. He crossed the river and explored the present states of Arkansas and Louisiana. As the party was returning in 1542 along the Mississippi De Soto died and his men buried him in the waters of the great river he had discovered. Although he had dissipated his fortune in a vain quest for riches, he accomplished a far worthier result in opening a vast territory for those who followed.

FROM THE PAINTING BY POWELL.

CORONADO IN THE SOUTHWEST

Led on by tales of seven cities to the north, each one as rich as the great one in Mexico found by Cortez, Francisco de Coronado with a large expedition turned northward from New Spain in 1540. He explored our southwest. He found Indians living in pueblos and saw buffalo, but no gold, and returned home. In thirty years the Spaniards, seeking wealth, had opened up Mexico and the Southern and Southwestern United States for the real work of colonization.

30

RALEIGH: QUEEN ELIZABETH COMMISSIONS HIM TO SAIL FOR AMERICA

Sir Walter Raleigh was the first man to visualize America as a place in which Englishmen might find homes, not wealth. He attempted to have Virginia colonized in 1584, again in 1585, and for a third time in 1587. This last expedition was led by John White, an incompetent who chose the poor soil of Roanoke on which to settle. He saw the colony launched and then hurried back to England for supplies and new settlers.

COURTESY FRICK ART REFERENCE LIBRARY.

CROATOAN

THE LOST COLONY

When White left, the remaining colonists promised that if they moved away they would leave behind them the name of their destination. In 1591, when he returned, the word "Croatoan," the name of a tribe of Indians, was found on a tree. The colonists had vanished. Years later the settlers learned they had gone to the Indians. If any escaped massacre they were doubtless absorbed into one of the Indian tribes, and a tradition to this effect has continued throughout the centuries. So ended the attempt to settle a colony in America.

SETTLEMENT IN 1607

In 1606 a better organized attempt was made to settle Virginia by the London Company. Advantage was taken of the mistakes at Roanoke, and a landing was made at Jamestown in 1607. The colony's sponsors in England decreed that it be ruled by a board of seven men, and the sealed document embodying this decree was opened just before landing. But it was an impossible type of government, and Edward Wingfield, one of the seven, soon was chosen president. The picture shows the arrival of a ship from England, bringing supplies and new settlers to the struggling colony.

SETTLERS IN JAMESTOWN

The new colony did not prosper. All profits from the venture were to go to the sponsors, the London Company, and so the powerful impetus of private gain was absent. Moreover, some settlers had little desire for work and were inclined to sit by while indentured servants performed the manual labor. Disease, idleness, and incompetence very nearly extinguished in its first years this fourth attempt by Englishmen to settle America.

34

35

THE LEGEND OF JOHN SMITH AND POCAHONTAS

By his energy and resourcefulness John Smith soon displaced Wingfield and became the acknowledged leader in Jamestown. On one of his expeditions to the Indians to barter for food Smith was captured. According to a tale told by Smith many years later, he was saved from death only when Pocahontas, daughter of the powerful chief Powhatan, begged for his life. Smith advanced the colony but when he sailed for England things sank back again, and the winter of 1609–1610 was known as the "starving time."

MARRIAGE OF POCAHONTAS

Although some doubt has been cast on the story of Pocahontas and John Smith, it is certain that this attractive Indian maiden was the first convert of her people to Christianity. She married John Rolfe, one of the early settlers. Many families still prominent in Virginia trace their ancestry to this marriage, including that of the Bollings, one member of which was the second wife of President Woodrow Wilson.

ATTACK BY THE INDIANS

It was Sir Thomas Dale, a harsh tyrant, who eventually set Jamestown on a permanent foundation. He forced the idle to work and ruthlessly killed those who shirked. In 1622 the Indians, seeking to protect their land, slaughtered four hundred settlers; and in 1644 three hundred more. In later years a system of great estates, so characteristic of the South, was to come into being, based on slave labor, the growing of tobacco, and still later, the growing of cotton.

JAMESTOWN SURRENDERS

The colony grew rapidly and by 1650 held more than 15,000 inhabitants. The long and prosperous tenure of Sir William Berkeley, although a proud and arrogant governor, had much to do with the changed conditions. One of his wisest decisions was to surrender peaceably in March, 1652, to a fleet sent over by Parliament. By this he not only saved bloodshed but also many of Virginia's charter rights.

BACON'S REBELLION: ASKING AID OF BERKELEY

In 1675 the colony was again menaced by Indian raids and the settlers on the borders came to Berkeley asking aid. He refused it and soon the people began to raise troops under Nathaniel Bacon. To Berkeley, this was treason. Bacon turned against him. He seized and burned Jamestown. On Bacon's death from fever the revolution collapsed, but it had shown how Virginians felt toward arbitrary emissaries of the king, and it was an omen of 1776.

SIGNING THE MAYFLOWER COMPACT

The Pilgrims, separatists from the Church of England, first went to Holland in their search for a place where they might worship according to their beliefs, but after ten years in that country, finding that their children were growing up to be more Dutch than English and not having prospered financially, they determined to settle in America. One hundred and two of them sailed in the first *Mayflower* in 1620. Before landing they signed the famous Mayflower Compact which looked towards the establishment of a democratic form of government for the colony.

THE LANDING OF THE PILGRIMS

The *Mayflower's* objective was Virginia but, sighting Cape Cod, the Pilgrims chose, after weeks of exploration, the present site of Plymouth for their home. On December 26th they came ashore. They were almost as poorly equipped to fight the wilderness as were the Virginians.

Their religion, an absolute faith in a literal reading of the Bible, together with their plain speech, plain clothes, and modest bearing, were, however, not unsuited to the trials ahead.

FROM THE PAINTING BY CHARLES LUCEY.

41

DEPARTURE OF THE "MAYFLOWER"

FROM "GREAT MEN AND FAMOUS WOMEN."

When the *Mayflower* sailed away the last tie with home was cut. The Massachusetts winter had set in and food was scarce. By spring, fourteen of the eighteen wives who had sailed in the ship died. When a good crop was eventually harvested a Thanksgiving Day was set aside to commemorate it. Governor Bradford's good sense in dealing with the Indians and in abolishing communal labor had much to do with saving the colony.

42

PILGRIMS GOING TO CHURCH

The colony at Plymouth, after the first few years, took on a semblance of permanence. Education was begun and, of course, attendance at church was the accepted thing. The Pilgrims were, however, far less militant in their religion than the Puritans who, in 1629 and 1630, settled the larger colony of Massachusetts Bay. They arrived in force at Salem, then Boston, and finally settled seven other towns. They were recruited from the business men of England and brought the instinct for trade with them to the new world.

FROM THE PAINTING BY GEORGE H. BOUGHTON IN THE NEW YORK PUBLIC LIBRARY.

SLAUGHTER OF THE PEQUOTS

As the colonies expanded trouble with the Indians was inevitable. In 1637, stirred by a common enemy, the whites joined against the Pequots in an inter-colonial war managed by the Massachusetts colony and the Connecticut towns. John Mason and John Underhill were the leaders. The Indians were cornered. Of some four hundred men, women, and children, only four escaped alive. The Pequot tribe was extinguished by this and a subsequent bloody slaughter which, although cruel, gained peace for the colony for many years.

JOHN ALDEN AND PRISCILLA

Miles Standish's gruff character as a soldier has lent credence to Longfellow's story of his courtship of the pretty Priscilla Mullins. It is a popular legend that the bashful Standish sent John Alden to court Priscilla for him and that she, knowing Alden's heart was not in his mission, suggested that he speak for himself. Alden did marry her, however. He lived to be the only surviving member of the original *Mayflower* company.

STOPPING A FARMHOUSE FROLIC

"Puritanism" in American life and letters has become a symbol of restraint. It placed a curb on the boisterous expression of natural good spirits, and was for many years a restraining influence on the social life of New England. Of great influence were the divines, John Cotton, and Cotton and Increase Mather. After their decline there was a lull until the fiery Jonathan Edwards stirred for the last time the dying embers of religious and semi-religious frenzy.

46

ENDING THE REVELS AT MERRYMOUNT

It must be remembered that the Puritans came to America not to set up a colony for free worship but to set up a home where they might worship as they chose. A corollary of this was their readiness to impose their ideas on others; and against Thomas Morton, a carefree adventurer, they discovered a dual reason for taking action. He was their rival in the profitable fur trade and soon felt the force of their righteous arms. One day they appeared at his settlement, tore down his gay maypole, put an end to his revels, and banished him to England.

ROGER WILLIAMS ARRIVES IN RHODE ISLAND

Roger Williams was another to fall afoul of the Massachusetts authorities. He was banished because, among other things, he maintained that to acquire land legally, the colonists must buy it from the Indians. Escaping from Massachusetts, he founded Providence in 1636, the first colony in which religious toleration became a reality. He made friends with the savages, and through this friendship, rendered valuable service to his late oppressors during their war with the Pequots.

FROM THE PAINTING BY ALONZO CHAPPEL.

ENDICOTT REMOVES THE CROSS

One of the most forceful personalities among the Puritans was John Endicott, rash, bigoted, and brave. He it was who first purchased from the Plymouth Company several miles of Massachusetts coast, extending westward to the Pacific, and settled Salem. He was both a leader in the Pequot War, and one of the chief persecutors of the Quakers. One of his exploits was the cutting of the cross from the king's ensign, even this symbolism being contrary to his scruples.

WHIPPING QUAKERS

The Puritans could not stem the rising tide of liberal thought in the colony, but they tried. First Mrs. Anne Hutchinson, a lady of fine birth, was banished for expressing her religious convictions, and the subsequent slaughter of her entire family by the Indians was considered a judgment of God. Next they turned on the Quakers, even putting some of them to death. Massachusetts was unique in the length to which it went in these persecutions.

THE SALEM WITCH TRIALS: A GIRL BEWITCHED

The darkest blots on early New England history are the witchcraft killings in Salem of 1691 and 1692. In all about thirty people, mostly friendless old men and women, were put to death, one by the horrible method of crushing with heavy weights. The evidence which was presented in court by those who claimed they had been bewitched made a mockery of English justice. The craze finally collapsed as suddenly as it had started.

HARVARD COLLEGE

Education was a primary concern of the New Englanders. In 1649 a law was passed requiring every town of more than fifty families to support a school. Meanwhile, in 1636 Harvard College, the only center of higher learning for half a century, had been founded. This view of early Harvard was engraved by Paul Revere who, thrifty soul, cut off during the Revolution the missing half of the plate that he might use the copper to engrave bank notes.

DUTCH AND ENGLISH QUARRELS IN CONNECTICUT

It was natural that with a colony started in Massachusetts, the English should spread to the rest of what they called New England. The Dutch were in what is now Connecticut before them, however, having planted a settlement at the present site of Hartford in or previous to 1633. The two were soon in conflict and quarrels were not uncommon. Temporary peace was established in 1650. The government established to the south differed in one important respect from that of Massachusetts in that there was no religious test for citizenship.

CULVER SERVICE.

THE FRANKLIN
HAND PRESS, 1725.
FROM THE GROWTH
OF INDUSTRIAL ART.

MAKING FELT HATS.
FROM THE GROWTH
OF INDUSTRIAL ART.

54

CATCHING, DRESSING. AND DRYING THE COD, FROM KEITH'S. VIRGINIA, 1738.

EARLY INDUSTRY

In the century and a half from the actual colonization of the new world to the outbreak of the Revolution, America passed through the first stage of her industrial development. The first settler and his wife had, of necessity, to make most of what they needed with their own hands. Gradually, as the social system crystallized and money began to circulate, there grew up a place for the skilled artisan. By the middle of the 18th century a high degree of commercial self-sufficiency had been attained. Although labor-saving devices (machinery) were beginning to make an appearance in England by 1790, it was not until after the War of 1812 that Americans made the first steps from artisan labor to the factory system.

WEYMOUTH ON THE KENNEBEC

There is no certainty as to who first discovered the coast of Maine. In 1605, however, George Weymouth was sent to "North Virginia" to maintain English claims of prior possession. He journeyed up the Kennebec River, the shores of which entranced him with their virgin beauty. Unfortunately for later settlers, and for the victims, he kidnaped several Indians whom he took back to England.

56

FROM THE PICTURE BY R. W. WEIR.

LANDING OF HENRY HUDSON

At about the same time that Virginia was being settled, the Dutch began moving into the area dominated by the Hudson River. They sent Hudson in 1608 to discover a northwest passage to China. This was much the same objective that led on the great company of early explorers, a century and more before. Hudson failed to find the passage and turning south at last entered New York Bay. In 1609 he sailed up the mighty river, named after him, to what is now Albany, and a small boat was sent even further. Hudson's discoveries proved that the river did not lead to China, that there was no isthmus in North America as there was at Panama, and led directly to Dutch colonization.

FIRST SETTLEMENT ON MANHATTAN

Hudson's explorations revealed the value of the river valley. The first houses on Manhattan sprang up around a trading post on the southern tip, established by the Dutch. In 1621 New Netherland was put under the newly chartered Dutch West India Company which sent out directors to govern it. In 1623 or 1624 about thirty Walloon families arrived, but all but eight of the men in the company continued up the river to settle Fort Orange, now Albany.

THE PURCHASE OF MANHATTAN

In 1626 Peter Minuit negotiated the famous purchase of Manhattan Island for cloth, beads, and other trinkets to a total value of about $25. The Dutch later made an attempt to transplant the patroon system to the region dominated by the upper Hudson, but feudalism in any form was unsuited to the wilderness. Although the number of colonists increased slowly, the town gradually assumed a prosperous, even a wealthy, air. The comfortable life of the traders of this era shaped its social and economic structure for many years after Dutch rule disappeared.

FROM THE PAINTING BY ALFRED FREDERICKS.   COURTESY OF THE TITLE GUARANTEE & TRUST CO.

PEACE WITH THE INDIANS

When Peter Minuit retired troublous times came to the colony. Governor van Twiller met opposition to Dutch expansion in Connecticut and along the Delaware. His successor, William Kieft, arriving in 1638, found himself faced with the necessity of arousing a sluggish population to fight the Indians. To conduct the war he imported John Underhill, one of the leaders in the Pequot War slaughters, from New England, and peace eventually was made in 1646. Kieft finally gave way willingly to Peter Stuyvesant, last and greatest of the Dutch governors. .

FALL OF NEW AMSTERDAM: STUYVESANT MARCHES OUT

Stuyvesant was stubborn, brave, hard-hearted, and possessed of a violent temper, but withal a good governor. He did more to improve the physical condition of the city than all his predecessors. The English, who had never given up claim to all the Atlantic coast, decided in 1664 it was time to eliminate the Dutch. A fleet appeared in the harbor and Stuyvesant, pegging up and down on his wooden leg, vowed he would fight. But the city was defenseless, the people were opposed to him, and he was finally led forcibly by them from the ramparts without a gun being fired. The Atlantic seacoast from Maine to Florida was in English hands.

CARTERET LANDING IN NEW JERSEY

With the fall of New Amsterdam, New Jersey was granted to the Duke of York and that same year he conveyed it to Lord John Berkeley and Sir George Carteret. Berkeley sold his interest to two Quakers. Later, one of these two disposed of his share to three Quakers, one of whom was William Penn. Later still, the three acquired the share of the other Quaker. The quinpartite deed of 1676 gave Carteret East Jersey and the Quakers West Jersey. Carteret's land was put on the auction block in 1682 and Penn and eleven associates bought it in for £3400. The twelve were later doubled in number and in 1701–2 all the proprietors surrendered their rights of jurisdiction.

PENN'S TREATY

In settlement of a debt owed to his father, Charles II gave William Penn a grant of land in the new world. In 1682 the young Quaker, fired with the idea of governmental and religious freedom, sailed up the quiet waters of the Delaware to take possession of his grant. The name Pennsylvania is the Latinized form of Penn's Woods. Almost Penn's first act was to make a treaty with the Indians, and his next was to establish for his colony a liberal form of self-government.

PENN'S COLONISTS ON THE DELAWARE

At the confluence of the Schuylkill and the Delaware River, Penn established Philadelphia, the town of "Brotherly Love," laying out an architectural plan of rectangular divisions bounded by broad straight roads or streets—a design which was one of the earliest city planning projects that later served as a model for many other cities throughout the world. All men who pro-fessed faith in Christ were invited to come there. English, Welsh, and Germans flocked to the new colony, and so rapid was the growth of Penn's "green country town" that it soon surpassed the older settlements of Boston and New York, becoming the foremost commercial center of colonial America.

FRANKLIN IN PHILADELPHIA

Franklin and Philadelphia. It was the "happy marriage" of our early history. The story of his arrival in the city as a poor boy with a loaf of bread under his arm is a true American legend. The secret of his success was his rare common sense and his ability to make others see a plain fact, plainly arrived at. He was a printer and publisher, an inventor, a scientist, a philosopher, a public-spirited citizen, and a statesman. Before he died he was hailed as the "wise man" of the new nation.

THE STATE HOUSE

Although the French and Indian wars upset the borders, life in and around Philadelphia continued peaceful and prosperous up to the Revolution, in comparison with the disturbances in the other colonies. Despite quarrels with Penn's heirs, relations with the proprietors in England were fairly amicable. The city's landmark was the State House (later Independence Hall), built between 1731 and 1751. In the additions to it, built in 1791, sat the Supreme Court and the Congress.

DE VRIES VISITS HIS RUINED COLONY

The Dutch colony established by David De Vries in Delaware was destroyed by the Indians in 1632. De Vries wrote that he found there only "the skulls and bones of our people." Other Dutch settlements followed and a conflict with the Swedes, who had also settled on Delaware Bay, ensued. Peter Stuyvesant conquered the settlements of New Sweden but in 1664, when New Netherland fell, Delaware also became English. Although the colony had an independent legislature it was governed by the chief executive of Pennsylvania, under the Duke of York's grant to Penn, down to 1776. Maryland, by reason of Baltimore's grant, did not release claim to all of Delaware until 1767, when the present dividing line between the two states was laid down.

LAYING OUT BALTIMORE

George Calvert, the first Lord Baltimore, obtained from James I a grant of lands near the James River where he thought he and other Catholics might find a haven of peace. The actual grant was issued to the son, Cecilius Calvert, in June, 1632. The "Charter of Maryland," containing the patents to the Lords Baltimore then and in future, was noteworthy in its guarantees of freedom of government, even freedom from taxation by the crown, and freedom of religion. Cecilius delegated command of the expedition to his younger brother, Leonard Calvert. He was accompanied by two Jesuit priests, Father Andrew White and Father John Altham, and in all about 300 emigrants. They sailed on November 22, 1633, in two ships, the *Ark* and the *Dove*, and landed in Maryland (named after the Queen) on March 25, 1634, the "day of the Annunciation of the Most Holy Virgin Mary"; they planted a great cross of wood and knelt around it while the litany was read.

FROM B. J. LASSING'S "OUR COUNTRY."

THE CAROLINAS: SETTLERS

Although some colonists had filtered southward from Virginia the settlement of the region between that colony and Florida was placed by the king in the hands of eight of his friends, who became the Proprietors. Two regions developed, bearing the names North Carolina and South Carolina. The latter, with important West India connections, the investment of greater capital, and the cultivation of rice and indigo on plantations worked by Negro slaves, became the richer and more aristocratic. North Carolina was relatively poor, and democratic. Both passed safely through the dangerous Indian wars. After much disorder, both colonies became royal colonies when the Proprietors sold their rights to the crown.

OGLETHORPE'S FIRST INTERVIEW WITH THE INDIANS

James Oglethorpe, moved by the wretched condition of the prisoners in English debtors' prisons, secured permission to start a colony in Georgia in 1733. There was also in view the idea of making the colony a line of frontier defence against the Spaniards to the south. This was the last unsettled land between Maine and Florida. Oglethorpe made peace with the Indians, forbade the introduction of slaves and rum, and limited the land holdings of each settler. These restrictions did not attract new colonists and prosperity was slow in coming until they were relaxed in 1749. Spain never had given up her claim to the southern coast and much of the time up to 1748, when the dispute was settled, was consumed with beating back the ambitious Spaniards.

SLAUGHTER OF THE FLORIDA HUGUENOTS

Although the Spaniards were the first to explore Florida they were slow to settle it. In 1564 De Laudonnière, the Huguenot leader, established at Fort Caroline a French settlement. The Spaniards realized that if their returning treasure ships were to be safe the land could not remain in enemy hands. Pedro Menendez was sent to rout the French. He not only routed them but butchered those who surrendered.

LAYING OUT ST. AUGUSTINE

Leaving a garrison at Fort Caroline, Menendez founded St. Augustine in 1565, the first permanent settlement in America. It has been said, though without satisfactory proof, that the French were not slow in dealing with their enemies. Dominique de Gourgues, suddenly appearing at Fort Caroline, killed all who resisted and hanged the prisoners. If this actually happened, it was an act of useless cruelty, for the French made no further attempts to expand there and Florida remained Spanish until it was purchased by the United States in 1819.

BUCCANEERS CAPTURING A SHIP

So long as Spain controlled the sea routes her treasure ships returning from the New World were relatively safe; but when the Spanish Armada was defeated, the pirates, English, Dutch, and French, began to intercept the stream of returning treasure. These picturesque murderers and highwaymen of the sea came from all stations in life. They flourished in the 16th century and on one occasion a pirate fleet is said to have captured at Vera Cruz booty worth $30,000,000.

73

VERRAZANO AT NEWPORT

Giovanni da Verrazano, an Italian, was the first to establish any French claim to the new world. He was sent out by Francis I in 1524 to find a route to China by way of a western waterway. Touching at about Cape Fear on the present coast of North Carolina, he sailed north. He discovered the Hudson River, and may have found the present Narragansett Bay, Newport harbor, and even the Gulf of St. Lawrence.

CARTIER AT HOCHELAGA

The voyages of Jacques Cartier were the real bases of French claims to Canada. In 1534 he set out to find the passage to China that had evaded so many others. That year and the next he explored the St. Lawrence as far as Montreal, where he visited the Indian village of Hochelaga. Aside from one abortive effort at Quebec in 1541 no serious effort at colonization was made until the coming of Champlain.

75

CHAMPLAIN SURRENDERS QUEBEC

Samuel de Champlain established Quebec in 1608, appreciating that that site was the key to the St. Lawrence River valley. He explored much of the country and made frequent trips to France to advance Quebec's interests. He was forced to surrender his beloved city to the English and the Iroquois in 1629 but when Canada was restored to French hands he came back to his post. His wife, whom he had married when she was but twelve, became a nun on his death in 1635.

CHAMPLAIN FIGHTING FOR THE INDIANS

One unwitting act of Champlain's lost the French all chance of expansion southward. He accompanied the Algonquins in a war party against the Iroquois in 1609. Two being shot by him, the Iroquois fled and the Algonquins roared with laughter at seeing their enemies so easily routed, but the French were henceforth to find the powerful Iroquois unalterably opposed to them in New York. On this trip Champlain discovered the lake named after him and in 1615 became the first white man to see the Great Lakes.

77

THE JESUIT BRÉBEUF

The arrival of the Jesuits gave impetus to expansion in New France. These fine men came to convert the Indians and to advance the fur trade for their country. They were successful with the Algonquins and the Hurons, but the Iroquois were implacable. Many of these French missionaries were killed, including Brébeuf, after excruciating torture. Following the Jesuits came the Ursulines, a teaching order, and the *Hospitalières* who were nurses. The Récollets were present before the Jesuits, but their ten years of missionary work convinced them that a richer, better organized group was needed to carry on.

RADISSON AND GROSEILLIERS IN THE WEST

Champlain was followed by Nicolet who explored westward to Lake Michigan. At one point in his journey, Nicolet, thinking he neared China, dressed himself in ceremonial robes. A quarter-century later Radisson and Groseilliers followed him and explored Lake Superior. Later, transferring their allegiance for a while to England, they were instrumental in establishing the Hudson's Bay Company's lucrative fur trade. The age of expansion, in which France claimed by right of original exploration all territory from Hudson's Bay to the Gulf and west to the Rockies, had begun.

JOLIET AND MARQUETTE ON THE MISSISSIPPI

That France failed to win all America except the coastal fringe of English colonies was, in the end, due to two factors. Too few settlers came to her settlements, and French sea power, the only method of communication with New France, was surpassed by the British. Two noted explorers of the Golden Age of exploration were Father Marquette, a Jesuit, and Joliet, a trader. They pushed beyond Lake Erie, descended the Mississippi to Arkansas in 1673, and then turned back fearing that the news of their great discoveries would perish with them at the hands of the Spaniards.

LA SALLE CLAIMS THE MISSISSIPPI

La Salle completed Marquette's work. Although undoubtedly a visionary he was the first to grasp the magnificent idea of a great French empire in the interior of America. In the time of the great Frontenac, the finest governor New France ever enjoyed, La Salle headed for the Mississippi which he appreciated was the key to his imaginary empire. He reached the Gulf in 1682 and, being assured by the Indians that he was the first white man to explore the river, claimed its valley for the king of France.

MURDER OF LA SALLE

The next year La Salle was in France. His plan was to settle Louisiana and an expedition was fitted out for him, but his ships, missing the delta, took him far to the west of the Mississippi. He spent the last months of 1685 in Texas vainly searching for his beloved river. He finally gave up and in 1687 turned north. His men were grumbling at the rigorous manner in which he ruled them, and finally one of the company killed him by shooting him in the back.

FRONTENAC: THE ATTACK ON QUEBEC IN 1690

Count Frontenac, a vigorous soldier, was France's opening gun in the battle for North America. Louis XIV sent him back to Canada as governor in 1689, for trouble with the English (King William's War) was just beginning. He carried out a series of bloody raids in New York, New Hampshire, and Maine. An expedition sent against him at Quebec in 1690 was a disastrous failure. Nevertheless the war dragged on for seven years. Neither side gained appreciably in this first trial of arms. It was the prelude to a struggle which was to continue for three quarters of a century.

PLAN OF ATTACK ON QUEBEC, 1690.[1]

[1] Fac-simile of an engraved plan in La Hontan's *New Voyages*, London, 1703, vol. i. p. 160. It was re-engraved for the French edition of 1705.

BIENVILLE'S ARMY ON THE RIVER

La Salle's work was completed by d'Iberville and Bienville. The former planted in 1699 the first trading post in Mississippi and the latter founded New Orleans in 1718. Both places had enormous possibilities which were never realized. Although Cadillac was to found Detroit in 1701 and La Vérendrye's sons possibly to see the Rockies in 1743, the great age of French exploration was over. The wars with the English and the Indians in the north put an end to the dream of a French empire on the Mississippi.

PORTOLÁ DISCOVERS THE GOLDEN GATE

The period which witnessed the decline of Spanish power in Europe saw the steady growth of her influence in southwestern America. Explorers and missionaries pushed their way into Lower California and then into California. An expedition under Don Gaspar de Portolá left San Diego in July, 1769, and a few months later emerged from the forest to see stretched below the great harbor of San Francisco Bay and the rock pillars of the Golden Gate.

85

PERILS OF OUR FOREFATHERS

Two basic conflicts were inherent in our colonial life, one between the settlers and the Indians (wars similar to that with the Pequots ravaged virtually all the colonies), and another between the English and the French. Both conflicts continued up to the eve of the Revolution. The French held Canada, including the St. Lawrence, and the Mississippi. They wanted the Hudson. The English wanted to push west. Where outposts of the two touched, only warfare could settle the issue.

KING PHILIP'S WAR: DEATH OF PHILIP

Philip, a Wampanoag, began the war that bears his name in 1675. The struggle was marked by ruthless slaughter on both sides, with complete annihilation of the enemy the one objective. Eventually the superior organization of the whites turned the balance. Although King Philip was killed in 1676, the struggle dragged on. During the fight the whites suffered serious losses of men, and great destruction of their crops and homes. but as a result the Indian menace in southern New England was removed.

ANDROS A PRISONER

Philip's war was no sooner over than another danger appeared. Charles II and James I intended to revoke the charter rights of the colonies and make them royal provinces. Connecticut, alarmed, hid her charter in an oak tree but even she submitted when Edmund Andros arrived in 1688 as the royal governor. His harsh rule, carried on in defiance of charter rights, was a short one, for when James was overthrown in England, the people rose and put Andros in jail.

88

PEPPERELL AT THE SIEGE OF LOUISBOURG:
KING GEORGE'S WAR

With King William's War, 1690–1697, began the serious conflicts with the French. It was followed by Queen Anne's War, 1701–1713, and King George's War, 1744–1748. In the first neither side gained, in the second the English won Acadia (Nova Scotia), Newfoundland, and Hudson's Bay. In the third William Pepperell captured the powerful fortress of Louisbourg, only to lose it under the unwise terms of the Treaty of Aix-la-Chapelle. These three wars were the prelude to the last act of the drama in which the curtain was to be forever rung down on the epic of French empire in the New World.

BRADDOCK'S DEFEAT

The last act of the drama of the struggle for North America, the French
and Indian War, was begun in 1754 with each side prepared to fight to a
decision. As a first move, the English sent General Braddock in 1755 against
Fort Duquesne. Near there his expedition was ambushed. His Virginia
troops fought as did the Indians, from behind trees, but Braddock forced
his regulars into solid files where they were excellent marks for the concealed enemy. He himself was wounded and about half his force was killed.
George Washington, already winning fame as a brilliant commander, played
a brave part in the retreat.

READING THE DECREE EXPELLING THE ACADIANS

The English now decided to make solid their hold on Nova Scotia, and the expulsion of the Acadians was agreed on. It is doubtful whether these farming people were a real menace but the English thought they were and, assembling them in their village churches, read to them the decree of expulsion. They were forced on ships and scattered heartlessly throughout the colonies. Longfellow has told a romantic story of this unnecessary brutality in *Evangeline*.

FROM THE PAINTING BY J. L. G. FERRIS. COURTESY GLENS FALLS INSURANCE CO.

MONTCALM STOPPING THE MASSACRE AT FORT WILLIAM HENRY

The year 1757 brought a serious English disaster. Fort William Henry had remained in English hands until that year, when its garrison marched out before Montcalm, the last great man in New France. Then the tragedy occurred. Montcalm could not restrain the blood lust of his Indian allies who set on the defenseless men. The French general risked his life to halt the slaughter, but at least fifty were tomahawked before his troops put an end to it.

92

WASHINGTON AT FORT DUQUESNE

The pace now quickened, for Pitt was in the saddle in England determined to force affairs, at long last, to a conclusion. A terrific bombardment forced the heroic defenders of Louisbourg to surrender to Lord Jeffrey Amherst in 1758. In New York, despite the catastrophe at Ticonderoga, Fort Frontenac was taken, and the same year Fort Duquesne was abandoned by the French to an expedition headed by John Forbes, in which Washington had a subordinate command. It was the beginning of the end, for both wings of the French dominions had begun to crumble, one on the Atlantic, the other on the Great Lakes.

FROM THE PAINTING BY I. R. CHAPIN.

DEATH OF WOLFE ON THE PLAINS OF ABRAHAM

At last the way was clear for the real objective of all this warfare—Quebec. Against it by sea came the greatest war fleet to cross the Atlantic up to 1917. Against it by land came eight thousand troops under General Wolfe. Montcalm, deserted by the government in Paris and harried by intrigue and corruption within the walls of Quebec, prepared to resist. Wolfe determined to make the decisive attack by land and on September 13, 1759, he fought the brilliantly conceived Battle of the Plains of Abraham. Both he and Montcalm fell, but Quebec was in British hands at last. Unparalleled scenes of celebration took place in London and the colonies. The next year Montreal fell and France laid down her arms in the new world forever. The dream was over.

PONTIAC UNITING THE TRIBES IN CONSPIRACY

Because the French were defeated, all was not yet safe for the ever-expanding English. Pontiac, as able an Indian as has ever lived, united the jealous tribes for one final effort, in 1763. Had he lived a hundred years earlier he might have succeeded. He led his followers to many victories but the end was never in doubt. Pontiac died at the hands of one of his own race who, for a barrel of rum, struck him down from behind. Pontiac's war showed London that the menace of the frontier remained. Ten thousand troops were accordingly kept in the colonies and it was planned to support them in part by the proceeds from the Stamp Tax, resistance to which was one of the links in the chain of events leading to the Revolution.

95

BURNING THE STAMPED PAPER

Several factors helped bring about the Revolution but one of the most important was the question of taxation. Parliament claimed the right to tax the colonies, while they resisted on the ground that they had no voice in the matter. In 1765 was passed, however, the Stamp Act. Instant and violent were the protests. The tax could not be, and never was, enforced. It was repealed in 1766 and by its very repeal British prestige suffered a severe blow.

THE "BOSTON MASSACRE"

No less irritating than taxes was the presence of 10,000 British troops in New England. To the claim that they were necessary for defense, the colonists asked why they had not been sent when protection was needed against the French and Indians. Whatever other reasons there may have been, the troops were in Boston partly to keep the hot-headed New Englanders in leash. Bloodshed was avoided for a time but in 1770, stung to fury by the taunts of the people, and finally one soldier being struck, a shot was fired. Before the trouble ended, five lay dead. The fat was in the fire. The average man understood the language spoken by bullets.

FROM THE PAINTING BY ALONZO CHAPPEL.

THE BOSTON TEA PARTY

After an effort at further taxation in 1767, designed to recognize a distinction between external and internal taxes, all these duties were repealed in 1770 except the tax on tea. Three years later Parliament passed another law which permitted the East India Company to export part of the tea stored in its warehouses free from all English duties, but subject to the tax levied for American ports. Part of this tea was about to be landed in Boston when on the night of December 16th a crowd of men dressed as Indians boarded a British ship and dumped its cargo of tea into the harbor. No taxed tea was wanted in Boston.

99

FIRST CONTINENTAL CONGRESS: DELEGATES LEAVING CARPENTERS' HALL

The rising tide of opposition to British rule finally brought about that which had never before been possible—sustained unity of action among the colonies. Hitherto, local jealousies and conflicting interests had kept them apart. Now, the rights of all were menaced. Virginia sent out the call for delegates to attend a Continental Congress. Philadelphia was chosen as a meeting-place, and on September 5, 1774, representatives of all but Georgia began sessions in Carpenters' Hall. The ablest leaders in America attended.

PATRICK HENRY IN THE FIRST CONTINENTAL CONGRESS

A radical party, not yet daring to broach independence, and a conservative element, for allegiance to the king, soon materialized. Despite this difference, resolves were passed in which the colonies claimed the right to legislate for their own affairs, and the rights inherent in personal and political liberty. Finally, a compact was made not to import from or export to Great Britain, after certain dates. With this, the Congress, which had served chiefly to unite the Whigs, adjourned.

PAUL REVERE'S RIDE

In the spring of 1775 Gage determined to break the gathering storm and dispatched troops to Concord, eighteen miles from Boston, to seize a supply of the colonists' military goods. Paul Revere, warned of this decision by a prearranged signal, a lantern hung in the North Church, rode through the night warning the farmers and the Minute Men, a body of militia formed but a few weeks before, of the coming of the British. He reached Lexington in time but was captured before he came to Concord.

FROM "HARPER'S WEEKLY," JUNE 29, 1867.

101

BATTLE OF LEXINGTON

In addition to the stores at Concord, the object of the British was the arrest of the radicals Samuel Adams and John Hancock. When the column arrived at Lexington shortly after dawn on April 19th, about a hundred militia opposed them. There was a shot, then a volley, and the colonials fled, leaving eight dead. The British lost not a man. The military significance of Lexington was infinitesimal, its political significance was, and still is, stupendous.

102

RETREAT FROM CONCORD

After Lexington the British pushed on to Concord and, covering the bridge, made a gesture at destroying the colonial stores. Those at the bridge were soon attacked by an overwhelming number of militia, the whole body being forced to retreat to Boston. The shot "heard around the world" had been fired and the Revolution had begun. During the retreat the red coats of the British made easy marks for the Americans, sharpshooting from farmhouse windows and from behind fences and trees. The finest British troops had been surrounded, ambushed, and outflanked. The wonder is that they escaped complete capture.

BATTLE OF BUNKER HILL

On June 16th the Americans fortified Bunker and Breed's hills overlooking Boston. Gage's besieged position in the city was now more than ever insecure. His troops attacked the next day but were twice driven back by the defenders who withheld their fire "until you see the whites of their eyes." Such was the practise of good frontier marksmen. On the third charge the Americans, their ammunition exhausted, retired. In the end the British carried the hill but the moral effect of the strong American defense, against able and well-trained troops, was great.

104

WASHINGTON TAKES COMMAND

War was now on in earnest and the army needed a general. Congress appointed George Washington, a gentleman from Virginia and a soldier trained in the Indian wars, to that position, and what had been a New England army became a Continental one. From the moment that he took command in Cambridge Washington never had a full quota of troops and was continually hampered by desertion and discontent. It was his patience, his firm hand, and the confidence and respect he inspired in men universally, as much as his ability as a commander, which brought the war to a successful conclusion six years later.

CAPTURE OF FORT TICONDEROGA

Now came one of those incidents which make the history of the Revolution so colorful. Ethan Allen of Vermont, on his own initiative, raised the "Green Mountain Boys," and proceeded against Ticonderoga. He surprised the garrison, and took the fort "in the name of God and the Continental Congress." The supply of guns, ammunition, and heavy cannon which he captured were desperately needed at Cambridge, especially the cannon which later played a part in taking Boston.

DEATH OF MONTGOMERY IN THE EXPEDITION AGAINST CANADA

Now came Benedict Arnold's daring march to Canada which although in the end a failure, came astonishingly near success. Its real objective was the winning of the Canadians to the American cause. Washington gave his full approval. Suffering incredible hardships, Arnold marched his men north through the approaching winter of 1775. Another column under Montgomery joined him after taking Montreal. Their joint attack on Quebec was a failure, Montgomery was killed, and Arnold retreated to Crown Point, contesting every foot of the way.

HOWE EVACUATING BOSTON

Meanwhile the British remained besieged in Boston. In the spring of 1776 Washington determined to bring the matter to a head. In a surprise move, he took Dorchester Heights. After that the city was at the mercy of the cannon captured at Ticonderoga. Lord Howe embarked his eleven thousand soldiers, together with the Loyalist inhabitants, and sailed for Halifax. He left behind him a prodigious amount of supplies and military stores which Washington greatly needed.

FROM THE PICTURE BY M. A. WAGEMAN.

108

STIRLING'S RETREAT AT THE BATTLE OF LONG ISLAND

After Boston, Washington marched to New York. The British plan was to capture the city, proceed up the Hudson, and so split the colonies in two. Washington, unwisely, decided to contest the issue on the heights of Brooklyn. There poor generalship accomplished his defeat on August 27, 1776. With his army in immediate danger of capture, Washington now brought about one of the most brilliant retreats in military history—the secret transfer of his entire army across the East River to Manhattan. He himself escaped with the last of the troops.

FROM A PAINTING BY ALONZO CHAPPEL.

EXECUTION OF NATHAN HALE

Nathan Hale's farewell words, "I regret that I have but one life to lose for my country," are part of our tradition. He was a young man. When the British occupied Manhattan, Washington was in continual need of knowledge about Howe's plans. Hale volunteered to secure this information. He disguised himself as a Dutch school-teacher and entered the city, but the British captured him and after a trial before Howe he was hanged as a spy.

FROM "HARPER'S WEEKLY," SEPTEMBER 30, 1876.

BATTLE OF HARLEM HEIGHTS

Washington's parting shot after abandoning New York was the Battle of Harlem Heights on September 16th which he won. There followed in rapid succession a defeat at White Plains, and the loss of Forts Washington and Lee. By these victories Howe gained control of the lower Hudson and had he pushed on he might have ended the war in late 1776, but he allowed Washington to escape and retreat across New Jersey to the south side of the Delaware at Trenton.

111

FROM THE "NEW YORK MIRROR," SEPTEMBER 24, 1842.

WASHINGTON CROSSES THE DELAWARE

Frederick the Great once said that Washington's successes between December 24, 1776, and January 4, 1777, were "the most brilliant" in military history. Moving quickly, he pushed his way through the ice-clogged Delaware, marched to Trenton through the sleety night, and early in the morning of December 26th captured the surprised town. Still moving fast he was back across the river before he could be caught, only to recross it again on the last day of the year. Then he struck, again with lightning speed.

112

BATTLE OF PRINCETON

Circling the enemy flank he fell on a large column at Princeton, routing it in the early morning of January 3rd. These victories stayed the desertions that were decimating his ranks and brought new recruits to him in the spring. After adroit maneuvering in New Jersey in the summer of 1777, Howe sailed for the Delaware but ended by entering Chesapeake Bay. Washington followed cautiously and south of Philadelphia on the Brandywine Creek on September 11, he was defeated in a battle which he should have won. Howe then invested Philadelphia.

113

FROM THE PAINTING BY E. H. CORBOULD.

MURDER OF JANE McCRAE

The Saratoga campaign of 1777, a sequel to Arnold's stubborn retreat from Canada, was a complete American victory. By this Burgoyne was prevented from joining hands with Howe in New York and so cutting off Washington's retreat through New Jersey. Schuyler, Lincoln, and Gates commanded the campaign, but Arnold played a large part in bringing about success. One act of some Indians, supposed to be allied with Burgoyne, helped to bring the militia flocking to the American side. This was the abduction and murder of Jane McCrae. Hearing of it, the population rose in arms on all sides.

114

ARNOLD WOUNDED AT SARATOGA

Burgoyne advanced slowly, his forces suffering successive defeats at Bennington, in the Mohawk Valley, and twice at Freeman's Farm. Indecisive action accomplished his defeat. He turned back on Saratoga but by now the Americans had him surrounded. On October 17, 1777, he surrendered his entire army. Success in this campaign was due more to the subordinates, Stark, Lincoln, Morgan, and Kosciuszko than to the commander, Gates. The American victory was the turning point of the Revolution. It is counted among the decisive battles of the world.

FROM THE PAINTING BY ALONZO CHAPPEL.

BATTLE OF GERMANTOWN

Washington was determined to surprise the British in Philadelphia. On a foggy morning in early October four columns marched on the city by separate roads. In Germantown the battle seemed won, but the British barricaded Judge Chew's mansion and there resisted Washington's main column stubbornly. The retreating troops rallied. General Greene's men, usually reliable, lost their way in the fog and then one of his subordinates, being intoxicated, caused the soldiers under him to fire into Wayne's troops. Washington's brilliant plan was a failure and he retreated to Valley Forge.

FROM THE PAINTING BY ALONZO CHAPPEL.

116

DE KALB INTRODUCING LAFAYETTE TO SILAS DEANE

When news of Saratoga arrived in Paris the task of securing a French alliance, assigned to Silas Deane and Benjamin Franklin, became easier. A promise of men, money, and ships was quickly made. Equally as important to the American cause were the volunteers, Lafayette, de Kalb, Pulaski and Kosciuszko, the Poles, and Von Steuben, a Prussian. Inspired by our struggle for independence they all rendered valuable service, especially the youthful Lafayette who became Washington's lifelong friend and confidant.

117

WASHINGTON'S TROOPS AT VALLEY FORGE

The winter at Valley Forge was Washington's low point. His rival, Gates, had received credit for Saratoga while he himself had done little but retreat and suffer defeats since Princeton. Congress now became critical of his military tactics. In addition, it failed to supply his men with food and clothing, many of whom fell sick and died in the rude snow-bound huts above the Schuylkill. Meanwhile, the British danced, wined, and slept peacefully in the comfortable city of Philadelphia. The bright spots in the winter were the budding confidence in Lafayette and the services of Von Steuben, the drill master. When spring came to the rolling Pennsylvania hills he had made well-disciplined soldiers out of the raw recruits.

BATTLE OF MONMOUTH

The British now left Philadelphia, Washington trailing them cautiously to Monmouth, New Jersey, where the two armies met on June 28, 1778. It was a blazing hot day. Charles Lee, in command of the attack, lost Washington the great opportunity for which he had been waiting, and for which Von Steuben, Lafayette, and Greene had labored in the dark days at Valley Forge—the capture of the British army or a large part of it. Lee retreated almost without having attacked. He was later dismissed from the army for his conduct. Monmouth was the last general engagement in the north.

FROM THE PAINTING BY C. F. BLAUVELT.

ARNOLD'S TREASON

With the British holding New York, American control of the upper Hudson was essential. That control was West Point and the command of it was given Benedict Arnold. He was a brilliant officer and on his record should have held a position second only to that of Washington. But Congress had both harried him and promoted over him men of less ability. Stung to the quick, Arnold persuaded the young British officer Major André to carry plans of the defenses at West Point to Clinton, the British commander in New York.

LAST MOMENTS OF MAJOR ANDRÉ

André was captured near Sleepy Hollow, and the papers found in his boot. Hearing of his capture, Arnold escaped from West Point and later fought for the British. André was hung as a spy, an act which the British claimed was murder, saying he should have been treated as a prisoner of war. Had Arnold resigned from the army his worth undoubtedly would have been recognized, and that in his own lifetime. Tradition says that, years later, as he was dying in London he called for his faded American uniform saying, "May God forgive me for ever putting on any other."

CLARK AT KASKASKIA

George Rogers Clark is responsible for the winning of the northwest.
"The Hannibal of the Missouri" is the historic name which he acquired
by his conquest of what was then known as the Northwest Territory.
With but two hundred men he took Kaskaskia and Vincennes in Illinois
but was forced out of the latter place. The little army then marched
back to Vincennes, sometimes wading through icy water that was neck
deep. Clark's one chance was to take the fort before reënforcements
would come to it in the spring. On February 24, 1779, the garrison was surprised. Clark's campaign pushed the British back to Detroit and made the
western country safe for the rest of the war.

CAPTURING THE "SERAPIS"

John Paul Jones, commanding the *Bon Homme Richard*, closed with the British ship *Serapis* on September 23, 1779, and when asked if he was about to surrender called back, "I have not yet begun to fight." The deck of the *Serapis* was cleared of defenders and she was captured. Jones established the tradition of heroism in the American navy. Next to Jones's exploits, the most important naval battles of the Revolution were fought by the privateers. They did British shipping much damage.

WASHINGTON IN THE TRENCHES AT YORKTOWN

FROM "HARPER'S WEEKLY," OCTOBER 22, 1881.

The British moved the war to the south in 1778 hoping to conquer the less solidly anti-Tory colonies and sweep north. This plan was ultimately unsuccessful. Wearied by long marches which won him small victories but no territory, Cornwallis at last retreated to Yorktown, Virginia. Now came to pass the opportunity so long awaited, to make use of the French fleet. De Grasse was prevailed on to cut off the possibility of either reënforcements or a retreat by water, French and American troops were hurried down from the north, and the "mouse trap" sprung.

124

SURRENDER AT YORKTOWN

Cornwallis was outnumbered two to one. About half of Washington's troops were French regulars. The end was inevitable. It came on October 17, 1781. When it was time to deliver up his sword on the 19th, Cornwallis pleaded illness and it was handed over by General O'Hara to General Lincoln who immediately handed it back to O'Hara. Everyone realized the war was over.

The peace treaty of 1783 recognized the independence of the United States with a boundary line, roughly stated, as the Mississippi, the middles of lakes Superior, Huron, Erie, and Ontario, the St. Lawrence, and then, with the exception of the northern part of Maine, the forty-fifth parallel to the coast. Spain held Florida.

FROM THE PAINTING BY JOHN TRUMBULL IN THE YALE SCHOOL OF FINE ARTS.

WASHINGTON AS COMMANDER

Time and historical research have only verified the popular American belief that the war was won by George Washington. With an inferior force given to deserting him each year as winter came on, with jealousy and conspiracy often within his own staff, and with a Congress continually insolvent and hence unable to give him adequate support in men and supplies, he held steadfast before the finest troops in the British army for more than six years. It was a man, no sentimental story-book hero who did this. Around his genius as a commander (great, but not as great as some would have it), his fairness, his ability to inspire confidence, and above all his rare charm, the Revolutionary War was accomplished.

JOHN HANCOCK

John Hancock played a leading part in Massachusetts before, during, and after the Revolution. He was rich and possessed of a high social position. Therefore when he championed the cause of the radicals, his words carried more weight than did the opinions of less eminent men. He was for revolt from the beginning, played a large part in winning the reluctant ones over to the Declaration of Independence, and later became the first governor of his state. Although his purse stood to profit by independence, commercial motives alone did not dictate his fight for liberty.

SAMUEL ADAMS

Samuel Adams was the organizer, the firebrand, and the drill master of the Revolution. At the age of 21, on receiving his master's degree from Harvard, he sounded the keynote of the Revolution, and that was 36 years before the Declaration of Independence. He was among the first to propose independence, he continually opposed compromise with England, and he directed the Boston Tea Party. He was a supreme politician and a master of impassioned appeal. He and Hancock were warned of the intent of the British to arrest them at Lexington and escaped before the battle took place there. He based his faith on the common man and never faltered in that faith.

COURTESY OF THE MUSEUM OF FINE ARTS, BOSTON. FROM THE PAINTING BY IOHN SINGLETON COPLEY.

128

PATRICK HENRY SPEAKING TO THE VIRGINIA ASSEMBLY

Patrick Henry, orator and statesman, was the idol of the common people of Virginia. Not quite as radical as the New Englanders, Adams and Hancock, he was yet one of the outstanding political figures of his day. As early as 1765 Patrick Henry stirred the House of Burgesses in aristocratic Virginia with his defense of the rights of British subjects and his defiant opposition to the Stamp Act. He ended his burst of oratory with the now famous words, "If that be treason, make the most of it." Standing in the doorway listening with rapt attention was a 22-year-old Virginian, Thomas Jefferson, who then and there was fired with the justness of the American cause and eleven years later wrote the Declaration of Independence. Patrick Henry has been aptly described by Claude G. Bowers as "the prophet, the phrase-maker, the orator, the trumpeter of revolt."

THOMAS PAINE: Pamphleteer

The idea of independence was at first foreign to the minds of the mass of American colonists. They struggled during the early years of the Revolution only for what they conceived to be their inalienable rights as English subjects. The popular movement for independence, the movement which converted the people generally to this radical step can, however, be dated from the publication of the little pamphlet *Common Sense* in 1776, written by Thomas Paine. Thousands read its simple, easy-to-understand words, and Washington himself paid tribute to its widespread effect. Paine's earlier and also tremendously successful pamphlet, *The Crisis*, had begun with the famous words, "These are the times that try men's souls."

THE ADOPTION OF THE DECLARATION

On June 7, 1776, Richard Henry Lee on behalf of Virginia offered the resolution "that these United Colonies are, and of right ought to be, free and independent states." John Adams seconded on behalf of Massachusetts. On June 11th Benjamin Franklin, John Adams, Roger Sherman, Robert R. Livingston, and Thomas Jefferson were chosen as a committee to prepare a Declaration. Though he was only 33 years of age and the youngest member of the committee, Jefferson received the most votes and therefore became the chairman. The committee left the task entirely to him and he wrote it at a single sitting without reference to any book or memoranda. Franklin and Adams then made a few slight alterations and then the committee presented it to Congress on June 28. The debate continued throughout the 2nd, 3rd, and 4th of July, when it was finally adopted and as Jefferson wrote in his memoirs, "signed by every member present except Mr. Dickinson." However, the only signed Declaration known to us was engrossed later and signed on August 2, 1776. This document bears the signatures of some who became members of the Congress after July 4th and it lacks the signatures of a few of those who voted for adoption.

READING THE DECLARATION OUTSIDE THE STATE HOUSE

"All men are created equal," "Life, Liberty and the pursuit of Happiness," "free and independent," "pledge . . . our Lives, our Fortunes, and our sacred Honour." Such were the words below which John Hancock was the first to place his name. As news of the Declaration spread throughout the colonies, many marked the event with public celebration, but others were left sobered and thoughtful by the solemnity of the words they read and the finality of the step that had at last been taken. There could be no turning back now.

131

Entered according to Act of Congress in the year 1874, by DAVIS GAREER, in the office of the Librarian of Congress at Washington, D. C.

Independence Hall, Philadelphia, on the Eve of July 4th, 1776.

EXPLANATION.—It is sunset on the 4th of July, 1776. The members of the Old Continental Congress, having signed the Declaration, are seen in the act of leaving the Hall of Independence. HANCOCK, distinguished by his dark dress, stands on the steps in front of the hall-door, announcing to a friend that the Declaration has just been signed. FRANKLIN is seen at his right, JEFFERSON leans against the right pillar of the door. ADAMS is conversing with Jefferson—between their heads is seen the face of LIVINGSTON, and against the left pillar stands ROGER SHERMAN. These form the group on the steps. We then commence on the left of the picture, and counting every figure, discover the following persons: 1, a citizen; 2, WILSON, a signer; 3, a citizen; 4, a tory; 5, a signer; 6, a lady; 7, her father; 8, the Indian who bore the Declaration to the camp of Washington; 9, Thomas Paine, talking with No. 10, BENJAMIN RUSH and 11, ROBERT MORRIS, both signers. Behind them the heads of citizens are seen and to the right, a crowd of patriots, Quakers, tories, &c., eagerly disputing the merits and merits of the Declaration.

BETSY ROSS AND THE FLAG

The popularly believed story of the origin of the first flag is open to very serious doubts. Betsy Ross was an upholsterer in Philadelphia. The story is that Washington and George Ross came to her asking if she would make a flag. They showed her a design, decided on five-pointed instead of six-pointed stars, and later sent her a colored design, following which she sewed together the flag. Certain it is that it was not until June 14, 1777, that Congress declared the flag should have thirteen stripes, alternate red and white, and thirteen white stars on a blue field.

FRANKLIN AT THE FRENCH COURT

Franklin, during the war, was sent by Congress to secure aid from France. The task was far from easy. He, a Protestant, at a Catholic court, was appealing to a sovereign to help a group of rebels overturn their own legitimate sovereign. In addition, the colonies had been the enemies of France for a century and a half, but the desire to check the increasing power of Britain prevailed and Franklin completed his mission, securing men, money, and ships. He became extremely popular in Paris (shopkeepers ran out to see him as he passed down the street), he went to Versailles frequently, and was received by Louis XVI and Marie Antoinette. When he died in Philadelphia in 1790, the French assembly went into mourning for three days.

133

SIGNING THE CONSTITUTION

When the war ended, far-sighted men soon began to realize that there was need for a stronger tie between the states. After four years of increasing financial embarrassment, difficulties as to commerce, and the appearance of unrest in some of the states, a group of conservative leaders arranged for the calling of a Constitutional Convention in Philadelphia in 1787. To it were sent, fortunately, the most able statesmen and leaders of the day. Washington presided, the venerable Franklin was present, and both exercised great influence. The opposition was fearful for the rights of the states. After violent controversy and many compromises the present Constitution was the result. The success and final accord "is one of the miracles of history. It was due to the genius and patriotism of a few men, and among these the foremost was James Madison." His own contemporaries gratefully named him "Father of the Constitution." On September 17, 1787, thirty-nine of the fifty-five delegates signed. But their action was taken in the name of the states present, i. e., represented.

CELEBRATING THE CONSTITUTION IN NEW YORK

Having won equal representation in the Senate, most of the small states hurried to adopt the Constitution. Two of the largest, New York and Virginia, lagged. Without them the union would indeed have been weak. Madison led the fight for adoption in Virginia and Hamilton in New York. In New York *The Federalist* papers, a series of essays explaining the Constitution, did much to win the popular vote, and finally she ratified in July, 1788. In the city there was a huge celebration parade in which moved the ship *Hamilton*, named for the chief author of *The Federalist*. When Rhode Island ratified in 1790, a stable form of government had at last been set up in America.

WASHINGTON INAUGURATED

It was the unanimous opinion of the country that Washington should be the first president. Only with reluctance did he accept the honor. His journey from Virginia to New York for the inauguration was a triumphal procession. He was sworn in on April 30, 1789, on the balcony of Federal Hall. Although perhaps not a great statesman he commanded, however, universal respect and was able to prevent the country from splitting into violent factions in the first critical years of its existence.

136

HUNTERS AND TRAPPERS

The hunter and the trapper have become symbols in our history. These people, in the vanguard of civilization, pushed the frontier across the Alleghenies, then to the Mississippi, to the Missouri, to the Rockies, to the great northwest, and to the Pacific. Carrying what little they owned in the world on their backs, they departed from their homes, leaving their more settled countrymen to struggle with the problem of turning thirteen loosely bound colonies into a united nation.

THE PIONEER WEST

The pioneers, who followed in the footsteps of the early hunters, brought their families with them. Their wives, after braving the hardships of the outward journey, settled down to make homes in the rude cabins their husbands built. They ate of the scanty food, did the cooking, made the family clothes, helped to fight off the Indians, thought little of raising families of ten children, and all this in continual poverty. Such was the caliber of the American pioneer stock. Who can say that they were not happy?

138

DANIEL BOONE: LEADING A PARTY THROUGH THE CUMBERLAND GAP

Daniel Boone has become the exemplar of the hunter-pioneer type—brave, resourceful, kindly, and always restless in the settlements. His life illustrates the era of westward expansion before and after the Revolution. In the spring of 1769 he stood gazing down on "his" Kentucky. Under the direction of Richard Henderson and Co., he helped to defend and establish the settlement of Kentucky. But the lands he chose for himself among his neighbors were, in the end, taken away from him because of a technical flaw in the legal title. Hence in 1799, when he was sixty-five, he left Kentucky again for the west. Far away on the Missouri River and alone once more he made his last home.

FROM A PAINTING BY CHARLES M. RUSSELL. COURTESY MONTANA HISTORICAL SOCIETY.

LEWIS AND CLARK: MEETING WITH THE SHOSHONES

Captain Meriweather Lewis and Lieutenant William Clark were the first to reach the Pacific by crossing the continent north of Mexico. One was the brother of George Rogers Clark, "The Hannibal of the Missouri," and the other was secretary to Thomas Jefferson, who inspired, counseled, and partially financed the expedition so that the recently acquired Louisiana Territory might be extended to the far northwest; assuring the American people a vast empire stretching from the Atlantic to the Pacific; wiping out the danger of conflicting bordering nations like those that have caused constant wars in Europe. They started from St. Louis in 1804 with the definite task of getting accurate information about the land and the Indians to the west. They made the difficult ascent of the Missouri River, crossed the Rockies, and then descended the Columbia River system to the ocean. Their discoveries constituted our most important claim to the Oregon territory.

140

ESTABLISHING TERRITORIAL GOVERNMENT AT MARIETTA

In 1787 Congress provided for a territorial government northeast of the Ohio River. Among other things this Ordinance, drawn by Thomas Jefferson, declared that slavery would not be tolerated therein. The Ordinance became the model for the other territories and states which were to come into being in the west. Immigrants at first came slowly into Ohio, but when the government opened new land offices in 1800 and allowed settlers to buy on credit at $2 per acre as little as 320 acres, the flood began.

THE FUR TRADE: SURRENDER OF ASTORIA

The fur trade was a potent factor in opening up the Far West, just as it had been in the East. John Jacob Astor, a New York capitalist, attempted to organize this trade. He planned to have his American Fur Company dominate the Great Lakes, the Western plains, and the northwest. His settlement at Astoria on the Columbia River failed. When the War of 1812 approached he sold out his property rights to the Northwest Company of Canada, and a little later a British squadron captured the settlement, but it was restored to the United States after the war. The other two ventures added to Astor's already large fortune.

SANTA FÉ TRADE

The route from St. Louis to Independence, and thence across Kansas to Santa Fé (the Santa Fé Trail), sprang into life after Mexico revolted from Spain. Cotton cloth and other manufactured articles were carried out to the Indians. Furs came back. The trade lasted up to the war with Mexico. Although there was ruthless competition between the traders, they banded together in caravans while crossing the Indian-infested country of Kansas.

FROM A PAINTING BY ALLEN TRUE IN THE PUBLIC LIBRARY, DENVER.

FROM "HARPER'S WEEKLY," FOR SEPTEMBER 4, 1858.

THE MORMONS AT SALT LAKE: THE DESERET STORE

In 1847 the Mormons (Latter-Day Saints) arrived on the shores of Salt Lake, Utah. There Brigham Young, his authority absolute, sought to set up his empire. More than 15,000 came to his tiny city. While the element of polygamy has received popular attention it must be remembered that Young was one of the great colonizers of history because by irrigation he made the desert produce. Furthermore, the stores which the Mormons set up, such as this one at Salt Lake City, did a thriving business with the weary California-seekers. In the latter part of the 19th century the Mormons made permanent peace with the United States and abandoned the practise of polygamy.

144

SETTLEMENT OF CALIFORNIA

As late as 1750 there was little knowledge of California. Spain had long occupied Lower California but it was 1769 before a real attempt was made at colonization to the north, and then mostly through the missions which grew to dominate both the Indians and the economic life of the country. After California broke with Spain in 1822 the missions were secularized. In the years before the Mexican War, Americans began moving in in large numbers, to trade and to find homes.

THE COTTON GIN

In 1793 Eli Whitney invented the cotton gin, a hand-operated contrivance for separating short staple cotton from its seeds. This machine transformed a part of our economic life. It made it possible for cotton-growing to flourish in the South, gave life to a social system centering around great estates, added another export crop to Southern agriculture, and made slavery a permanent institution. Slavery and cotton were the answers to the problem of developing the post-Revolution South.

146

THE ERIE CANAL

The nation and its goods moved along roads in the years immediately after the Revolution. In the 1820's and 1830's, however, water transportation was on the increase. It was the success of the Erie Canal from Buffalo to New York which after 1825 gave the "Canal Era" its impetus and lifted New York to economic leadership. Many cities sought to benefit themselves by building canals. The railroad put an end to the great era of canal construction.

147

FULTON'S "CLERMONT"

Our natural waterways began to play their great part in American history
with the coming of the steamboat. Robert Fulton's *Clermont* chugged out
into the Hudson River in 1807 amid the cheers of a crowd that had come to
jeer at the inventor and his "folly." Fulton put nothing new into the steamboat. His great achievement was to assemble for successful commercial
use parts which others had developed. In providing cheap transportation
his invention had enormous economic implications.

148

COMING OF THE RAILROADS: THE FIRST TRAIN IN PENNSYLVANIA

The railroad was destined to have the greatest effect of all on our economic life. The locomotive, an English invention, began to supplant horses on American railroads in the early 1830's. First the Baltimore & Ohio experimented, then the Charleston & Hamburg, and then the Mohawk & Hudson. As the success of this new means of transportation became apparent many small roads sprang up all over the country. After the Civil War began the era of consolidation.

Matthias W. Baldwin

Inventor and Builder of Locomotive Old Ironsides

PHILADELPHIA GERMANTOWN & NORRISTOWN RAILWAY DEPOT

P.F.GOIST DEL.

FIRST RAILWAY TRAIN IN PENNSYLVANIA,

Drawn by "Old Ironsides" on the Phila., Germ. & Norr. R. R.

FIRST TRIP, 23rd NOVEMBER, 1832.

AGE OF THE CLIPPERS:
THE "FLYING CLOUD"

FROM "GLEASON'S PICTORIAL," MAY 31, 1851.

Americans had always known how to build good boats and sail them, but after the War of 1812 American ships began to be a force in world trade. The financial success of the lines operating packets, ships that sailed on a regular schedule, worked this change. They captured the cream of the Atlantic trade. But competition was stiff and the cry was for more speed and yet more speed. In 1845 John Willis Griffiths gave his answer. He launched the first clipper, the *Rainbow*. On her initial voyage to China she not only paid for herself but re-turned her owners a profit equal to her cost. Griffiths became a hero. One of the greatest clippers ever built was John McKay's *Flying Cloud*. She reached San Francisco in eighty-nine days, a record never beaten by a sailing vessel. The record for a clipper's single day's run was and still is 436 miles, made by *Lightning*, a mark that rivals many modern steamers. The years of the clippers marked the zenith of our merchant marine. In their day the finest ships the world had ever seen flew the American flag.

GROWTH OF NEW YORK: BROADWAY AT ST. PAUL'S CHURCH, 1831

Our cities were the first to feel the effects of the changes wrought by the new inventions, the cheaper transportation, and the spread of our population. As one instance, the Erie Canal may be cited. Its opening in 1825 marked the beginning of modern New York as a financial and industrial center. Such things were an indication of the tremendously important fact that the country's economic prosperity was beginning to find a basis in pursuits other than those of agriculture.

GROWTH OF CHICAGO: THE FIRST SHIPMENT OF WHEAT

The decade of the 1830's witnessed Chicago's birth as a city. A tiny village in 1830, by 1840 she had seen her destiny clearly. From her harbor her first shipment of wheat, seventy-eight bushels, was sent in 1838. A railroad connection with the East in 1852 gave her a firm grip on the already enormous lake trade and helped to establish her as the center of a fertile territory rich in natural resources.

THE AGRICULTURAL SOUTH

In the years before the Civil War the South developed its unique social system. The great slave-owning planters, who were but a fraction of the white population, dominated this system. Next was the great bulk of the white population, who owned their farms but few slaves.

The slave population grew from about 650,000 in 1790 to almost four million in 1860. By and large the South shared in the economic progress of the rest of the country.

GROWTH OF ORGANIZED RELIGION

The first years of the 19th century witnessed a revival of the religious spirit. The English church, loyal during the Revolution, was reorganized on an American basis. The Methodists spread rapidly through the work of the itinerant preachers. Puritanism was disintegrating by 1800 and from its ashes eventually rose the Unitarians and other sects that dissented from the old form. The period also witnessed the rise of the camp meeting, that unique American institution. It became a powerful influence in the religious life of the rural sections. The illustration shows the Old North Church in Boston, one of the most famous of the early New England places of worship.

GROWTH OF ORGANIZED EDUCATION

The much-prized system of public schools, so universal today did not come into existence at an early date. In Virginia a state-wide school system was proposed in 1779 by Thomas Jefferson in his "Bill for the General Diffusion of Knowledge," but it was not until 1825 that he succeeded with a part of the program with the opening of the University of Virginia. In Massachusetts it was not until the work of Horace Mann, during the 1840's, that education became universally available. The middle states between 1815 and 1860 gradually perfected school systems, but in the South good schools for everyone did not come until after the Civil War. However, there was wide public education almost from the first in the West. The period witnessed the rise of the Academy, the founding of many colleges and universities, and the beginning of the great state university system, first in the South, then in the Southwest and West.

COURTESY OF THE INTERNATIONAL HARVESTER CO.

THE FIRST TESTING OF THE McCORMICK REAPER

Cyrus McCormick perfected a reaper in 1834. After ventures first in New York and then in Ohio he began to realize that the tiny city of Chicago was the key to the vast grain fields of the prairies where the market existed for his invention. To that city he moved in 1847 and began selling his machine on the installment plan, an idea almost as revolutionary as the invention itself. The reaper gave the Mid-West farmer his place in the economic sun and his fields became the granary for both this country and a large part of Europe.

156

THE MORSE TELEGRAPH

Samuel F. B. Morse made the first telegraph instrument in 1836 but it was not until several years later that the doubting world gave him a chance to show what he had done. Meanwhile, he suffered poverty and rebuffs here and abroad. At last Congress passed an appropriation with which a telegraph line was built from Baltimore to Washington. On May 24, 1844, the famous message, "What hath God wrought," was tapped out and the instantaneous transfer of human thought became an accomplished fact.

DIGGING GOLD IN CALIFORNIA

The story of the gold rush to California in 1849 and 1850 is the story of a country gone crazy. News of the first discovery turned San Francisco into a deserted city almost over night. Five hundred ships soon lay in the harbor without sailors, and newspapers suspended publication because there were no typesetters. More than twenty thousand persons set out overland from the east, suffering innumerable hardships and risking life itself in the search for easy riches. Thousands more arrived by water.

FROM "BALLOU'S PICTORIAL DRAWING-ROOM COMPANION" FOR MAY 3, 1856.

158

FROM "GLEASON'S PICTORIAL," 1851.

JENNY LIND SINGING IN CASTLE GARDEN

Jenny Lind was almost unknown here when P. T. Barnum, hearing of the furore she had created in London, decided to risk his fortune and bring the "Swedish Nightingale" to New York. Her first concert at Castle Garden, in September, 1850, was attended by a huge crowd. On learning that someone once paid $225 for a ticket she wrote home naïvely, "It is amazing what heaps of money they have here." Almost every appearance during her tour of our cities was in the nature of a civic event.

159

THE "AMERICA" READY FOR LAUNCHING

In 1851 the schooner *America* sailed for England to accept a challenge that had been sent to American sportsmen by the Royal Yacht Squadron. She had been built by a syndicate of New York yachtsmen. On August 22nd she beat seventeen of the fastest boats in England on the difficult course around the Isle of Wight, her nearest competitor being twenty-four minutes behind. The cup that the *America* won has been successfully defended for almost eighty-five years against all comers.

FROM "GLEASON'S PICTORIAL" FOR MAY 31, 1851.

PERRY OPENS JAPAN

In 1854 Japan, sleeping in self-imposed isolation since time immemorial, was opened to the world by Commodore Matthew C. Perry of the American navy. Perry, backed by six vessels and bearing a letter from President Fillmore, concluded with the *shogun* our first treaty with Japan. This provided, among other things, that our ships should be permitted to trade in two ports and that privileges allowed other countries must thereafter be accorded to us. The photograph, taken at Washington in 1860, shows the first Japanese embassy to the United States.

FROM "HARPER'S WEEKLY" FOR SEPTEMBER 11, 1858.

THE ATLANTIC CABLE

Cyrus W. Field's attempt to lay an Atlantic cable in 1857 failed. In 1858, after another failure, his two ships met in midocean and, splicing a new cable, one sailed for Europe and one for America. Tremendous celebrations followed when the vessels reached shore. This contemporary drawing shows a miniature *Niagara*, one of the cable ships, being paraded in triumph on Broadway in New York. Field's joy was short-lived, for a month later the wire ceased to carry messages. Success, however, was ultimately attained in 1866.

162

THE PONY EXPRESS

The short-lived Pony Express is one of the most picturesque episodes in our history. It started April 3, 1860, between St. Joseph, Missouri, and Sacramento, California, a journey which it made in eleven days. Men changed horses every twenty-five miles and each man made three stages, except when Indians or bad weather forced a different schedule. As the telegraph lines advanced, the Pony Express cut down its run, and when the wires were joined in 1862 it became a memory.

163

THE FIRST BANK OF THE UNITED STATES

The first Bank of the United States, begun by Hamilton in Washington's first administration, occupied this building after 1796. The bank's charter had been the foundation for the famous controversy between Jefferson and Hamilton over the construction of the powers of Congress under the Constitution. The bank continued until 1811. Its charter expired in that year. The attempts to renew the charter brought about some of the political battles of President Jackson's administration.

THE FEDERALISTS AND THE REPUBLICANS

The campaign of 1796 was the first in which there had been a contest for the Presidency. It was marked by bitter party strife between Washington's Federalist Party and the Republican opposition. John Adams, a Federalist and a keen student of government but a poor politician, was elected. Thomas Jefferson, receiving the second largest number of votes, became Vice-President. He was the leader of the Republicans. The difficulties of domestic politics were aggravated by the fact that England and France were at war and that the government of the United States was thought by the French government to be bound to it by the treaty of 1778. James Monroe, appointed by Washington as minister to France, nevertheless sympathized with the views of Jefferson and his party and was, therefore, greatly embarrassed by the negotiation by Mr. Jay of the treaty of 1794 with Great Britain, which was, of course, most unpopular in Paris. Towards the end of Washington's administration Monroe was recalled and Charles Cotesworth Pinckney was sent over. But he was refused permission to reside in France. In the administration of John Adams the Federalists heard of this rebuff and became loud in their cry for war. Finally, after Pinckney had been succeeded by a commission and that commission had met in France offers of bribery, even some Republicans joined the Federalists in the popular slogan of the day, "Millions for defense, but not one cent for tribute." (The above illustration, which is contemporary, pictures the Federalist point of view in the controversy.) But Adams was able to restrain the hot-headed ones in both parties, partly due to the fact that France herself did not desire war. The differences were finally patched up in 1800, but party conflict had been intensified by the affair and in 1801 Jefferson, the first of the Virginia Dynasty, a believer in the common people and a clever politician, became President. The Federalist Party now entered upon its progressive decline.

The Cannibals are landing

THE WHISKY REBELLION

The Whisky Rebellion is significant because it came as a result of the first attempt to enforce federal laws in the states. In 1791 Congress had placed an excise tax on spirits, which the local whisky distillers in Pennsylvania resented. Violence began in 1794, and some federal officers who attempted to collect the tax were tarred and feathered. The 15,000 troops that Washington requested were more than enough to suppress the revolt, and this unneeded demonstration of power caused wide resentment against the Federalist party. Some said that Alexander Hamilton deliberately forced the tax as a test of federal strength.

JAY'S TREATY OF 1795

John Jay was sent by Washington to London to endeavor to settle the problems which had developed in our relations with Great Britain as a result of the outbreak of the great European war that followed the French Revolution. These problems included the searching of American ships on the seas, and the abandonment of the English outposts in the west, held by the British in violation of the treaty of 1783. The treaty he brought back. although it averted war and settled the question of the western posts, failed to reach a desirable settlement of the West India trade problem. It caused resentment against the Federalists. Jay was burned in effigy in many cities. The election of 1796 was, accordingly, a close one. Washington retired from office with his famous plea for freedom from European entanglement. John Adams became President.

THOMAS JEFFERSON AND THE REPUBLICANS

In 1801 the long reign of the Federalists came to an end with the election of Thomas Jefferson. Although a Virginia aristocrat, he however knew the reactions of the mass as Washington, Hamilton, and Adams had not. His principles of human rights, equality, economy, and states rights have become so fundamental in American politics that no wise candidate since his time has dared ignore them in word, however much they may have been able to avoid them in deed or by subterfuge.

CELEBRATING THE PURCHASE OF LOUISIANA

The greatest achievement of Jefferson's administration was the purchase from Napoleon of the Louisiana territory in 1803. By it our domain was increased by 140%. The acquisition made the entire Mississippi Valley completely ours and included most or all of thirteen future states. All possibility of war on our western border was abolished and the nation at last became free to exploit the vast territories and immense wealth of the country dominated by the mighty Mississippi.

169

THE BURR–HAMILTON DUEL

Aaron Burr, originally a Republican, joined the extreme Federalist party in
New York in the campaign of 1804 and so became party to an ill-starred
plan to split off the northern colonies from the union. Alexander Hamilton,
a Federalist himself, but loyal, bestirred himself to defeat his traditional
opponent. Burr, after the election, demanded satisfaction for some of the
charges made against him in the campaign, and the famous duel was the
result. Hamilton was killed and Burr fled for his life.

BURR ADDRESSING HIS ARMY

In 1805 Burr made his first journey to the west. Later, on the Ohio River, he began to hatch a scheme which was aimed either to establish a state of his own in Louisiana or to make an attack on Mexico. Just what he had in mind we may never know. In November, 1806, Jefferson ordered his arrest on the charge of treason, and his trial was the most sensational the country has ever witnessed. It was really a contest between Chief Justice John Marshall who presided, and who wished to establish the power of the federal courts at the expense of the executive, and Jefferson. Jefferson won, despite the fact that Burr was acquitted.

CULVER SERVICE.

INFLUENCE OF JOHN MARSHALL

John Marshall dominated the Supreme Court from 1801 to 1835. In a series
of famous cases he moulded the Constitution in its most plastic days along
conservative lines. He gave to the federal government much-needed
strength, and weakened the doctrine of states rights. Time and again the
people showed at the polls that their views were not those of the Chief
Justice, but he ignored them and by so doing strengthened the Constitution
as the basis of our national life.

172

MISSOURI COMPROMISE: RUFUS KING

Everything seemed peaceful in the Republican administration of Monroe (the fifth held by the "Virginia Dynasty" of Jefferson, Madison, and Monroe), until the suggestion was made that slavery be barred from the proposed state of Missouri. Instantly pandemonium broke loose. Finally, a compromise which it was hoped would settle the slavery question for all time, was agreed on in 1820. Missouri should come in without restriction, but henceforth slavery should be prohibited north of Missouri's southern boundary in the rest of the Louisiana Purchase. At the same time Maine was admitted, which helped satisfy the North. Rufus King, one of the recognized leaders of the Federalist Party, was an outstanding figure in the senate debates on the Compromise, supporting the anti-slavery side of the argument.

173

JAMES MONROE: THE MONROE DOCTRINE

The Monroe Doctrine came partly as result of the vaguely formed desire in Europe to regain for Spain her South American colonies. This did not suit England's ambitions and she suggested that we join in preventing it. Monroe had the sound advice of Thomas Jefferson and of John Quincy Adams, Monroe's Secretary of State; they had far too much sense to fall for any such scheme. Monroe announced in 1823 the so-called Monroe Doctrine. It embodied three ideas. First, we intend taking no part in European domestic troubles; second, Europe's political system, being different from ours, we would view as an unfriendly act any attempt to extend that system to American states which have established their independence; third, the American continents are not "subjects for future colonization by any European powers." This third principle was evoked by the threat of Russian expansion on the coast.

THE RISE OF THE TARIFF

With the act passed in 1816, the tariff became one of the battlegrounds of American politics. In 1824 a relatively moderate measure was passed due to the fact that some New England states were still anti-tariff. But in 1828 this division between the northern states had largely disappeared and with this unanimity a higher tariff wall was raised. The subject was soon a national issue, with the South in revolt. Calhoun became its spokesman in a movement which had important implications. The picture shows the Coffee-House Slip at the foot of Wall Street, New York, into whose harbor was already beginning to move the commerce of the world.

175

WEBSTER'S REPLY TO HAYNE

Calhoun became the chief sponsor of the doctrine of nullification, that is, that a state has the right to ignore the acts of Congress when that state deems them passed outside the powers granted by the Constitution or passed to affect but one section of the country. In 1830, as a result of a proposed limitation on the sale of public lands, Robert Y. Hayne, of Calhoun's own state of South Carolina, rose to defend the doctrine of nullifica- tion and states rights. He represented the flower of Southern oratory. A few days later, Daniel Webster of Massachusetts rose in reply. The gallery was crowded as he delivered one of the most masterly defenses of the Constitution ever conceived. After that, the debate sub- sided. Not even the most far-sighted men of the day saw that the issue was not settled.

176

ANDREW JACKSON'S "EXPERIMENT"

With the advent of Andrew Jackson in 1829 came "Jacksonian Democracy." He believed that the government had been run by the few for their own profit and set about to right the matter. The mass of the people was to be relied on. As a result of championing their cause, the people in their turn became suddenly willing to turn over to him immense powers of government. President Jackson's opponents called him "King Andrew" and claimed that the people were really robbing themselves. The cartoon, expressing the opposition to Jackson, shows the President as complete master of his ship. One of the sailors is saying, of the ship in the background, "There is the old *Constitution* burning up in the background"—Her owners having no further occasion for her and can't afford to keep her in repair."

THE SECOND BANK OF THE UNITED STATES

The charter of the first Bank of the United States, which had rendered yeoman service in straightening out our tangled financial affairs after the period of the Confederation, expired in 1811 and was refused renewal. In 1815 Madison, a Republican, asked for its re-establishment. It was said that he was out-Federalizing Federalism, for Jefferson had been most forceful, to Washington, in his opposition to the first charter. Monroe, the last of the Virginia Dynasty, followed Madison and under him the Bank prospered. However, in the first administration of Jackson, the Bank became the center of one of the severest political controversies in our history. Jackson, "the People's Champion," viewed the Bank as one manifestation of the power of the few over the many and he set out to destroy it. He accomplished this first, by vetoing a bill for the rechartering of the Bank and, secondly, by the simple method of not depositing any more funds in the Bank and by gradually withdrawing present governmental funds to state banks. (See the illustration, a contemporary cartoon.) In the controversy, Jackson was pitted against Nicholas Biddle, of Philadelphia, President of the Bank. Jackson was completely triumphant, and when the Bank's charter expired in 1836 it was forced to become a state bank. A chain of events following the end of the Bank and the distribution of the Treasury surplus, including the inflation of state bank notes, speculation especially in government lands, and finally the Specie Circular which required that all payments to the government be made in national currency, marked the prelude to the severe panic of 1837.

THE DOWNFALL OF MOTHER BANK.

Drawd off from Natur by Zek Downing, Neffu to Major Jack Downing.

HENRY CLAY: THE "FORCE BILL"

In pursuance of the doctrine of nullification South Carolina by ordinance of her convention in 1832 declared the federal tariff acts not binding on her. The situation became threatening when Jackson sent to Congress a bill empowering the President to enforce federal laws with the army and the navy. Henry Clay now removed South Carolina's objection by securing the adoption of a bill to reduce gradually the tariff. Having won her point, that state agreed to repeal her ordinance. Nullification was at an end. The country breathed easily again.

THE PANIC OF 1837

The panic of 1837 was one of those recurrent crises, the causes of which are still disputed. As is always the case, partisan efforts sought to blame the hard times on the party in power. In 1837, especially, the international aspects and influences were largely overlooked. One of Jackson's policies which later became an object of attack was specie payment. When it became obvious that paper issued by the state banks, which the government had received in payment for lands in the West, would not be redeemed in specie, Jackson ordered the government's land banks to receive no more of it. The collapse of the speculation in Western lands was one of the manifestations of the panic. The illustration is from one of the specie cartoons of the period immediately after 1837.

"TIPPECANOE AND TYLER TOO"

Jackson forced Van Buren on his party in 1836. No sooner had the latter become President than the panic of 1837 engulfed him. Failure of Van Buren really to cope with it accomplished his defeat in 1840. The Whig candidate, Harrison, the hero of Tippecanoe, won easily with Tyler as running mate, on the famous slogan, "Tippecanoe and Tyler Too." But in little more than a month after he took office he died, and Tyler, a Jeffersonian Republican, became President. The cartoon illustrates the popular conception of the result on election day.

THE ANNEXATION OF TEXAS

The election of 1844 turned largely on the question of the annexation of Texas. The Democrats, with Polk as a candidate, favored it. The Whigs opposed it, with Clay as their leader. Northern dislike of the spread of slavery in so great a territory figured largely. Polk's election decided the issue and Tyler hurried to secure the new state, which accepted the terms offered in the last days of 1845. Mexico meantime declared that the admission of Texas would be equivalent to a declaration of war. The cartoon shows Polk welcoming Texas, with Clay protesting.

THE TARIFF AND THE ELECTION OF 1844

The tariff was another of the battlegrounds of the bitter and exciting campaign of 1844. In Pennsylvania, Polk was openly accused of being a free trader. He cleverly answered this charge by saying he favored a tariff that would yield enough revenue for government expenses, if economically managed. This pleased the South and held protectionist Pennsylvania to her traditional political faith, for the tariff of 1842 had been passed to help defray government expenses. Pennsylvania Democrats campaigned for Polk on the slogan pictured in the cartoon.

THE OREGON QUESTION: A CARTOON

The westward spread of the population made the question of our right to Oregon an issue in the early 1840's. In pursuance of an agreement made in 1818 the territory had been occupied jointly by England and the United States, but in 1844 the West adopted the slogan, "Fifty-four forty or fight." It referred to the parallel up to which the extremists felt we had claim. England now compromised on a boundary along the forty-ninth parallel, the present line, and a settlement was made on this basis in 1846. Vancouver Island, in its entirety, went to Great Britain.

CALIFORNIA AND CLAY'S COMPROMISE

The rapid development of California and the rise there of a demand for statehood found Congress unable to pass necessary legislation by reason of unwillingness of Southerners to accept the Wilmot Proviso, which would exclude slavery. There arose danger of a secession movement, to avoid which Clay, whose powers for compromise had previously been manifested, brought forth conciliatory proposals in his Omnibus Bill of 1850. This was unsuccessful, but the same principles were enacted in separate laws. The tendency to disunion was postponed.

THE STRUGGLE FOR CANADA: CAPTURE OF FORT GEORGE

England had been high-handed in searching American vessels seeking to trade with the French, but this could have been settled amicably had not the West cast loving eyes on Canada and the fur trade. Madison yielded. We were forced to surrender Detroit in 1812 and then in early 1813, pursuing the campaign with more vigor, captured Fort George on Lake Ontario. Our opening move in the War of 1812 was against Canada.

BATTLE OF CHIPPEWA

The balance of the year 1813, although it brought victory at the battle of the Thames under Harrison of Tippecanoe fame, and the recapture of Detroit, did not lead to general victory. In July, 1814, two victories, one at Chippewa and the other at Lundy's Lane, were won but the campaign against Canada was abandoned. The treasury was now bankrupt and there was little public enthusiasm for Madison's war.

PERRY AT THE BATTLE OF LAKE ERIE

Naval victory on Lake Erie played no small part in the Canadian campaign. No progress could be made on land until the control of the water was established. On September 10, 1813, Captain Oliver H. Perry defeated an inferior British fleet, despite the fact that he lost his flagship the *Lawrence* and was only able to renew the fight after being rowed across to the *Niagara*. His brief message to Harrison, "We have met the enemy and they are ours," has become a classic in American naval history.

BATTLE OF PLATTSBURG

In 1814 the British began the invasion of the Lake Champlain country. On September 11th the two fleets met, while the land forces awaited the outcome. The American commander Thomas MacDonough now won the most daring naval victory of the war. By it he made safe an entire section of the frontier from invasion and quite counterbalanced British successes around the Niagara and the coast of Maine.

THE "CONSTITUTION" AND THE "GUERRIÈRE"

The history of the War of 1812 should have taught us for all time the futility of a tiny navy, however efficient, in protecting a great coast line. The series of thrilling naval duels between the frigates in which we carried off the honors, including the victory of the mighty *Constitution* over the *Guerrière* on August 19, 1812, and the defeat of Lawrence in the *Chesapeake* ("Don't give up the ship"), had little effect on the outcome of the war. The weight of the British navy accomplished the blockade in 1813 and from that time on our navy was ineffectual.

190

AMERICAN PRIVATEERS: THE "CHASSEUR" AND THE "ST. LAWRENCE"

War was no sooner declared than American privateers were in action. These rough-and-ready individualists effectively harassed British shipping, seizing prizes to a value of almost $40,000,000. One of their most dramatic duels was that between the *Chasseur* and the British warship *St. Lawrence*, near Havana, in which the latter was taken in fifteen minutes. They rendered great service but they drew many fine seamen from the navy and never coöperated for any general purpose such as the lifting of the blockade. This war was the last in which we resorted to their use.

THE BURNING OF WASHINGTON

The British in 1814 sent an expedition against Washington and Baltimore. They met but a few thousand badly trained and poorly officered militia. The city was easily taken and the Capitol, the Congressional Library, President's house (the occupant had fled), and executive offices ruthlessly burned. Baltimore was more stoutly defended, and the bombardment brought forth Francis Scott Key's "Star-Spangled Banner." If the naval blockade showed the futility of a tiny navy, however efficient, the sack of Washington showed the incompetence of a poorly trained militia. Madison had to withstand a storm of indignation.

ANDREW JACKSON AT THE BATTLE OF NEW ORLEANS

Andrew Jackson was the hero of the defense of New Orleans in 1815. His tremendous energy and great common sense made him a successful soldier and President, for both of which careers he was untrained. The British were contemptuous of the American militia. They had reason for this. They made the mistake, however, of underestimating Jackson's ability. He drove them off, saved the mouth of the Mississippi, and restored the faith of the people in their fighting ability.

TREATY OF GHENT

Negotiations for peace began in 1814. Neither side gained by the terms.
The searching of our ships and the impressment of our sailors, for which
we had gone to war, were not even mentioned. The Canadian border was
left for adjustment by a commission. The treaty was signed the day before
Christmas, 1814. When Jackson's men ceased firing at New Orleans on the
following January 8th, a peace that has lasted ever since began between the
two English-speaking nations.

WAR WITH TRIPOLI: DECATUR'S EXPLOIT

A war with Tripoli was brought on in 1801 by the practise of the Barbary states of demanding "presents" (tribute) for the privilege of trading in the Mediterranean. Our navy gained valuable fighting experience in the war and acquitted itself with honor. Tripoli eventually gave up her demands. An outstanding act of bravery in the war was Stephen Decatur's entrance in 1804 on a ketch into the harbor of Tripoli, and the firing of a captive American ship.

BATTLE OF TIPPECANOE

Under a treaty made in 1809, which some of the Indians, including Tecumseh and his brother The Prophet, denounced as illegal, the whites began moving in large numbers into Indiana. Tecumseh raised the tribes in opposition. Some of them surprised William Henry Harrison at Tippecanoe in 1811 but were forced to retreat by his overwhelming force. The trouble was a prelude to 1812, for the Indians had been aided by Canada. Harrison was undeservedly hailed as a great conqueror.

FROM THE PAINTING BY ALONZO CHAPPEL.

THE BLACK HAWK WAR: BATTLE OF BAD AXE

Tecumseh in 1811 had had some chance of success, but Black Hawk in
1831, not appreciating that the day of the Indian in the old northwest was
over, had none. His pathetic attempt to win back his lands on the eastern
bank of the Mississippi, from which he had been dispossessed, stirs the
admiration. He was defeated with ruthless slaughter at Bad Axe in 1832,
and he was himself taken prisoner and paraded through the streets of our
cities like a circus animal.

197

THE SEMINOLE WAR: OSCEOLA

When in 1833–1835 it was proposed to remove the
Indian inhabitants from Florida, the Seminoles under
a gallant half-breed leader rose in revolt. By his
ability to escape to swamps when closely pressed,
Osceola spread terror and death throughout the
country and always escaped capture. Eventually he
was treacherously seized under a flag of truce, but
the war dragged on until 1842 when the remnants of
his warriors consented to be shipped away.

THE TEXAN REVOLT: FALL OF THE ALAMO

The American inhabitants of Texas rose to a man in 1836 when Mexico showed an intent to limit their political rights. At the old fort of the Alamo a small band of less than two hundred was surrounded by Santa Anna. The defenders held out for thirteen days (some say eleven), when, all but a handful being dead, the place was taken by storm. News of the heroic defense and murder of the six survivors roused the memorable cry, "Remember the Alamo." Uniting under Sam Houston, the Texans, helped by sympathetic volunteers from the states, lured Santa Anna far northward to his destruction at San Jacinto in April. The American continent has not witnessed braver fighting than in the Texan revolt.

BATTLE OF BUENA VISTA

The Mexican War began in 1846 as a result of the annexation of Texas. General Zachary Taylor moved first into northern Mexico. He gained the strongly fortified town of Monterey and then, although handicapped by the fact that half of his army had been sent to Vera Cruz, won the battle of Buena Vista on February 22–23, 1847, completely defeating Santa Anna. He became the hero of his country and the following year was elected President.

THE CALIFORNIA EXPEDITION: FRÉMONT RAISES THE EMBLEM OF THE BEAR FLAG REPUBLIC

The second offensive movement in the war was planned against California. Colonel Stephen W. Kearney was directed to march overland to that territory, with the object of taking and holding the land now embraced by New Mexico, Arizona, and California. He had gone as far as Santa Fé when the guide, Kit Carson, brought him news of events on the coast. John C. Frémont, an army officer engaged in a supposedly peaceful tour of exploration in California, had lent himself to the movement known as the Bear Flag Republic. He figured in the military activities which that move for freedom from Mexico brought on, until he was sent back to the United States for court martial. His course in California's break from Mexico has ever since been subject to varying interpretations. By the time Kearney arrived, Mexico's influence in California's affairs was not large.

THE MEXICANS EVACUATING VERA CRUZ

The war was not won by the victories in California nor in northern Mexico but by Winfield Scott's brilliant march to Mexico City. He secured the surrender of Vera Cruz, then by fierce attacks took the strong positions of Cerro Gordo, Molino del Rey, and Chapultepec. On September 13, 1847, he stood before Mexico City. The next day the capital surrendered. The war was won. Despite some feeling that we should demand all of Mexico we settled on approximately the present boundary, which gave us New Mexico and California.

LIBERTY. THE FAIR MAID OF KANSAS—IN THE HANDS OF THE "BORDER RUFFIANS"

THE KANSAS–NEBRASKA ACT

When in 1854 it was proposed to make a territory out of the Nebraska country, the nation again realized that the slavery issue was not dead. It was only sleeping. Stephen A. Douglas now secured the passage of the famous Kansas-Nebraska Act with its doctrine of "popular sovereignty" (sometimes called "squatter sovereignty"), i.e., the people of each territory, when making their state constitution, are to decide whether it be free or slave. The Act repealed the Missouri Compromise, and was the first link in a chain of events which led to the Civil War.

203

AN ILLUSTRATION FROM "UNCLE TOM'S CABIN": LITTLE EVA READING THE BIBLE TO UNCLE TOM

In the campaign of 1856 the book *Uncle Tom's Cabin*, by Harriet Beecher Stowe, played an important part in making Buchanan's margin of victory a narrow one. His opponent was Fremont of California fame, the first Presidential candidate of the Republicans. The book was an impassioned protest against the fugitive slave law and although it overdrew the misery of the slave, thousands in the North put it down with the conviction that something should be done to remedy an inhuman situation. The book helped prepare the North, psychologically, for war.

DRED SCOTT DECISION: CHIEF JUSTICE TANEY

The Dred Scott decision of the Supreme Court in 1857 showed the North that a peaceful solution of the slavery question was not to be had by judicial decision. In this momentous case the court, of which Roger B. Taney was Chief Justice, held that not only was a slave property but that the Missouri Compromise was unconstitutional, and no Negro could plead in a United States court as a citizen. It was a complete rebuff for the anti-slavery party. Scott, a Negro, based his plea for freedom on the claim that a two-year residence in free territory made him free. Following the decision Northern aid and assistance to fugitive slaves became more and more widespread and open.

205

THE LINCOLN–DOUGLAS DEBATES

The debates that Lincoln and Douglas held throughout Illinois in the contest for the senatorship in 1858 showed the country clearly something that it vaguely sensed but which it hesitated to put into words. Lincoln had put it into memorable words in June, 1858, before the convention which nominated him for the senatorship: "A house divided against itself cannot stand . . . it will become all one thing or all the other." By this extreme statement which he knew was true and which he dared state openly for the first time he lost the senatorship but won the presidency, for he convinced the North. The most important question in the debates themselves was expressed when Lincoln asked Douglas, "Can the people of a United States territory in any lawful way, against the wish of any citizen of the United States, exclude slavery from its limits prior to the formation of a State Constitution?" If Douglas had answered, "No," he might not have been elected senator. He chose to answer, "Yes," and thereby greatly increased the difficulty in his nomination by the Democratic Party in 1860, because the answer revealed to the South the fallaciousness of Douglas's doctrine of popular sovereignty. Thus was forged another link in the chain leading to war.

JOHN BROWN'S RAID: BROWN LED OUT FOR EXECUTION

John Brown's raid on Harper's Ferry, Virginia, in 1859, caused a shudder to run through the South. Brown was an irresponsible fanatic but his attempt to raise the slaves and arm them against their masters had enormous consequences. During Brown's trial and execution he bore himself with remarkable fortitude and so became a hero in Northern eyes. The South was now convinced that many in the North were determined not only to deprive them of their property but to do it by arming their human property.

JEFFERSON DAVIS INAUGURATED

The chain of events which began with the Kansas-Nebraska Act reached its end when Abraham Lincoln was elected President in 1860. The radical secessionists in the South, who had split the Democratic party and nominated Breckinridge, while the conservatives nominated Douglas, realized that the time had come, and justified themselves by reason of the election of the President by a party unnecessarily sectional. It was now or never. In February, 1861, South Carolina, Georgia, Alabama, Mississippi, Louisiana, and Florida (Texas, Arkansas, Tennessee, North Carolina, and Virginia later followed) met at Montgomery, Alabama, and established the Confederate States of America. On February 18th, Jefferson Davis became President.

208

ABRAHAM LINCOLN INAUGURATED

Between election day in 1860 and inaugural the following March, the nation held its breath, waiting. Would Lincoln save the Union or let the Southern states secede? The tall man from Illinois, on whom all eyes were turned, slipped secretly into Washington to take the oath of office and deliver his inaugural address. It held the answer to the fatal question. Kindly, he stated he would defend the Union and preserve the Constitution he had just sworn to support. But it was too late to do this peaceably.

FROM "FRANK LESLIE'S ILLUSTRATED NEWSPAPER" FOR MARCH 16, 1861.

BOMBARDMENT OF FORT SUMTER

Even now each side hesitated to strike the first blow. But it was soon to come. When Lincoln ordered ships to go to the relief of Fort Sumter, within the boundary of the Confederacy, the Southern agents who were in Washington arranging for the fort's surrender and for recognition, went home. On April 12th the order to fire on the fort and its federal flag was given. After a thirty-four-hour bombardment Sumter surrendered. War had begun.

STONEWALL JACKSON AT THE BATTLE OF BULL RUN

The cry in the North soon became "On to Richmond." It was a fine idea but one not to be realized for four bloody years. At Bull Run near Washington, on July 21, 1861, the raw Union troops were checked in their rash advance. Here Thomas J. Jackson won his nickname, "Stonewall." The Northern retreat became a rout when the troops tangled with the carriages of congressmen and their wives who had driven out from the Capitol to see the great victory.

FROM A PAINTING BY H. A. OGDEN. COPYRIGHT, 1900, JONES BROS. PUBLISHING CO

211

FROM "THE ILLUSTRATED LONDON NEWS" FOR DECEMBER 7, 1861.

THE "TRENT" AFFAIR: THE "SAN JACINTO" STOPS THE "TRENT"

Throughout the war the South strove to win English recognition for the Confederacy. It never came and its failure contributed to defeat. The mass of the English people were unsympathetic to slavery and this, basically, decided the issue. In 1861, however, England and the North came near blows when the American ship *San Jacinto* seized on the high seas the British ship *Trent* on which were Mason and Slidell, two Confederate emissaries journeying to Europe.

BATTLE OF SHILOH

In the early days of the war the Southern troops had the advantage. Both Davis and his military adviser, Robert E. Lee, were West Pointers. Lincoln knew nothing of military art. The South recognized the ability of the Southern aristocracy to command and its troops obeyed them willingly, making good soldiers; while the untrained men of the Northern cities brought a spirit of independence into the trenches ill-suited to military discipline. The North, however, had the advantage of numbers, wealth, and natural resources. These factors, in the end, turned the tide. It must be remembered that the Confederate leaders never thought of capturing or conquering the North. They hoped, at best, to prevent the North from accomplishing the far more difficult task of conquering them, and they nearly accomplished their purpose. The military history of the war divides simply into two parts, a western and an eastern campaign. The object of the first was to win the Mississippi Valley, and then strike at the heart of the Confederacy from the west. The first great battle in the war was at Shiloh, on April 6th and 7th, 1862. It was also the opening gun of the western campaign. Ulysses S. Grant won his first major success, pushing the enemy back to Corinth in Mississippi.

FALL OF VICKSBURG

The Confederacy now lost Memphis and New Orleans. Vicksburg was the one strong point left them on the river. If it fell, Texas, Arkansas, and Louisiana would be cut off from the Confederacy. Grant now came south from Tennessee and by fine generalship cut off Vicksburg and began a siege which ended, after stubborn resistance, on July 4, 1863. The day before, the Battle of Gettysburg had been won in the eastern campaign. The North was jubilant.

BATTLE OF MISSIONARY RIDGE

General William Rosecrans, having won the Battle of Chickamauga in September, occupied Chattanooga and awaited Grant's arrival. The Confederates, under Braxton Bragg, occupied the heights of Lookout Mountain and Missionary Ridge outside the city. On November 24th and 25th the energetic Grant gave battle. William T. Sherman pushed back one wing, while Joseph Hooker took the mountain. Then George H. Thomas's troops, against orders, charged the center of the ridge, taking the crest. All of Tennessee had now been captured, and Atlanta was threatened.

SIEGE OF ATLANTA

Grant now became commander-in-chief, leaving Sherman in charge of the west. By a series of clever flanking movements executed through the summer of 1864, Sherman forced Joseph E. Johnston and then J. B. Hood back on Atlanta, which was evacuated in September. When he later began his march to the sea, Georgia "howled," as he said it would. This march split the Confederacy, but the same end might have been accomplished without the destruction he spread in his wake.

FROM "BATTLES AND LEADERS OF THE CIVIL WAR" BY JAMES E TAYLOR.

SHERMAN'S SOLDIERS FORAGING DURING THE MARCH TO THE SEA

Sherman dealt the South a blow which it was never to forget. He reached the seacoast at Savannah in middle December. In February, 1865, he turned north, spreading even worse destruction than in Georgia. His object was to join Grant against Richmond, but he was not needed there. The job of the western army was over. With inferior forces the Confederacy had contested every foot of its advance, only laying down its arms when exhausted by overwhelming forces.

FROM "HARPER'S WEEKLY" FOR JULY 26, 1862.

FIGHTING AT MALVERN HILL DURING THE SEVEN DAYS' BATTLE OF THE RICHMOND CAMPAIGN

The story of the eastern campaign is far different from that in the west. The North tasted defeat frequently, and once the cause of union came near destruction. It was marked by one futile attempt after another to find a competent general, a problem that was not solved until Grant's ascendancy in 1864. The first major move after Bull Run was again against Richmond, a campaign which George B. McClellan commanded and which culminated in the Seven Days' Battle, June 26 to July 1, 1862. The campaign failed, not because some battles were not won but because Joseph E. Johnston and Robert E. Lee halted, in the end, this attempt to take Richmond from the coast side.

BATTLE OF ANTIETAM

In late August at the second battle of Bull Run the Confederates, under the able generals Lee, Jackson, and James Longstreet, inflicted a crushing defeat on John Pope, the new commander. Lee then struck into Maryland. McClellan, replacing Pope, met him at Antietam, on September 17, 1862, in the bloodiest day of the war. Lee lost 11,000, McClellan 12,400. It was a Union victory and Lee recrossed the Potomac, but McClellan, failing to pursue him diligently, lost his command.

THE PROCLAMATION OF EMANCIPATION

Lincoln waited for a victory to proclaim the slaves in the rebel states free. Antietam in September, 1862, gave him his opportunity. Emancipation was proclaimed soon after, to become effective January 1, at which time a final proclamation was put forth. From this were omitted Tennessee and parts of other states, where the Union forces held control. The South did not observe it, but from then on, in addition to preservation of the Union, the war was waged for the abolition of slavery. The Thirteenth Amendment, constitutionally abolishing slavery, was ratified in 1865, and the conquered states accepted it after the war.

BATTLE OF CHANCELLORSVILLE

General A. E. Burnside now became commander of the Army of the Potomac. On December 13, 1862, in another attempt on Richmond, he lost the battle of Fredericksburg. The North was in despair. The energetic Hooker now replaced Burnside. He met Lee and Jackson at Chancellorsville on May 2 to 4, 1863. It was the last great Confederate victory. The three days' fighting lost both sides a total of 30,000 men. Stonewall Jackson fell, shot by mistake by his own sentinels.

FROM A PAINTING BY H. A. OGDEN. COPYRIGHT, 1900, JONES BROS. PUBLISHING CO.

JEB STUART'S RAID

Lee now decided to invade Union territory, hoping that a victory would induce the North to make peace. He started in early June, 1863, and so adroit was the work of his cavalry under J. E. B. Stuart that it was days before Hooker perceived what was afoot. Stuart now made one of the raids for which he was noted but which was, on this occasion, disastrous. He dashed behind the Federals, reached Carlisle, Pennsylvania, only to arrive at Gettysburg with exhausted men and horses.

222

BATTLE OF GETTYSBURG

The Union forces, now commanded by George Gordon Meade, followed Lee north. In Gettysburg, Pennsylvania, on July 1, the advance divisions of both armies met and joined battle. The day ended with a Union retreat, with the Confederates on Seminary Ridge, and their opponents frantically digging in on the rise of ground opposite, made by Culp's Hill, Cemetery Hill, Little Round Top, and Big Round Top. The fighting on the 2nd pushed both of Meade's flanks back. He assumed, rightly, that next day the attack would come on the center. George E. Pickett's division led that attack on the afternoon of the 3rd. Standing in front of Seminary Ridge, a mile from his objective, he began the advance. For a quarter of a mile he was protected, the rest was open ground. Across it came the grey lines, wave on wave, meeting and passing through a murderous fire. At last the Union lines were gained. For some few minutes the outcome was in doubt, then Pickett's men wavered. Back across the open space they went. The high tide of the Confederate arms left its mark on Cemetery Hill. Lee retreated to Virginia.

LINCOLN'S GETTYSBURG ADDRESS

Four months passed and the President came on November 19th to Gettysburg to dedicate the cemetery where lay buried men of both sides. In one brief page of remarkable prose Lincoln spoke his philosophy. ". . . that we here highly resolve that these dead shall not have died in vain, that this nation under God shall have a new birth of freedom, and that Government of the people, by the people, for the people, shall not perish from the earth."

224

BATTLE OF THE WILDERNESS: ATTACK AT SPOTTSYLVANIA

Both armies rested after Gettysburg. Grant became commander in March, 1864. His campaign was designed to crush Lee by sheer numbers. He fought the drawn Battle of The Wilderness in early May, then flanked and met Lee again at Spottsylvania Court House from May 8th to 21st. Again he was checked, but he wrote back, "I propose to fight it out on this line if it takes all summer." Again and again he flanked, losing some battles, winning no conclusive ones, but forcing Lee back to Richmond, to which he laid siege.

LEE RIDING TO APPOMATTOX COURT HOUSE

In early April the doomed city of Richmond fell, but Lee fled west. Grant followed. The end came on April 9, 1865, at Appomatox Court House. Even the brave Lee could hold out no longer. When the two great generals met to decide the terms of surrender, Grant won Lee's affection by allowing him and his officers to keep their side-arms, and his troops their horses. Said Lee, "It will be very gratifying and do much toward conciliating our people." Had Grant's generosity and Lincoln's magnanimity been displayed by those soon to direct the nation, the sad story of the reconstruction years would not have been.

226

BLOCKADE OF THE SOUTH: THE "MONITOR" AND THE "MERRIMAC"

The most important naval part of the war was the blockade of the southern coast. The Confederates, in 1862, constructed the iron-clad *Virginia* (earlier, the *Merrimac*), in an effort to break the blockade. On March 9, 1862, having had one day of glorious destruction, she met the *Monitor*, "a raft with a cheese-box on it." The battle was fierce and the *Virginia* retired. It marked the end of the hey-day of the wooden war ship.

CAPTURE OF NEW ORLEANS: BOMBARDING THE FORTS BELOW THE CITY

While the Union forces were recuperating after Shiloh, David G. Farragut undertook to capture New Orleans by water. It was a brilliant but dangerous plan, for the approach to the great Southern city was guarded by two strong forts. After five days of bombarding the forts Farragut decided to run between them. Early in the morning of April 24, 1862, he started. Once his flagship, the *Hartford*, went aground and was dangerously near destruction. Eventually his fleet passed through the heavy cross-fire from the forts. Once past them, the forts were cut off from assistance and surrendered. New Orleans surrendered soon after. The victory had profound moral effects in both North and South, and also on feeling toward the South in Europe, where the city was well known, especially to the French.

RAIDERS: THE "KEARSARGE" AND THE "ALABAMA"

Some ships escaped the blockade. Most famous of these was the Confederate raider *Alabama* under Raphael Semmes. She took, in all, thirty-six vessels. At last, at Cherbourg, France, on June 19, 1864, she was cornered by the *Kearsarge*, but bravely gave battle to her more heavily armed opponent. Not only was the *Kearsarge* heavier but she carried cleverly concealed chain mantlets protecting her engine room. Round and round the two ships fought, starboard to starboard. Finally the *Alabama* struck, then plunged downward, stern first.

FARRAGUT ON THE "HARTFORD" AT MOBILE BAY

Farragut was the outstanding naval commander of the North. On August 5, 1864, he won his great victory at Mobile Bay. Passing the forts commanding the harbor, he concentrated on the powerful ram *Tennessee*. Shot from ship after ship struck her armored sides without effect. Finally, her steering gear disabled, she surrendered. The victory put an end to blockade-running in this section and cheered the North, which was then reading the death lists of Grant's campaigns in Virginia.

LINCOLN AS PRESIDENT

From first to last, Lincoln's aim was to preserve the Union. That idea dictated his policy, military and political. As the war progressed he led the country as no other man has ever done. His character, in which honesty and sincerity prevailed, enabled him to do this. In March, 1865, he assumed office for the second time, and with it the problems of reconstruction. It is to him that today we owe a unified nation. The photographs show how his face changed in the four years between his first and second inaugural.

231

ASSASSINATION OF LINCOLN

Said Lincoln on April 14th: "I hope that there will be no persecution, no bloody work after the war is over." That night, in Ford's Theater, Washington, demented John Wilkes Booth shot him through the head. Booth leaped from the Presidential box to the stage, breaking his leg. That he then turned, shouting "*Sic semper tyrannis,*" is probably untrue. Booth was killed on April 26, while trying to escape, and his co-conspirators hanged, but that did not remedy the terrible blow his bullet had dealt the nation, especially the South.

RIOTING DURING RECONSTRUCTION DAYS IN NEW ORLEANS

People differed violently as to how the South should be brought back into the Union and the Negro given civil status. President Andrew Johnson was for a moderate policy, involving the minimum of humiliation. But the radicals in Congress, under Thaddeus Stevens, soon overpowered him, set up military governments in the South, and insisted that the Negro have all the civil rights of white men. Violence was inevitable. The controversy proved again that the habits of generations cannot be changed by legislative act.

FROM "HARPER'S WEEKLY" FOR AUGUST 25, 1866.

ECONOMIC RUIN OF THE SOUTH: FEEDING THE POOR

The war left the South prostrate. Every business and banking institution that had done business with the government was bankrupt or nearly so. Soldiers returned to barren fields or to bread lines in the cities. To all these woes were added the acts of the radicals in Washington. The whites soon came to believe that nothing more except death could happen. So grew up the "Solid South," dominated by a deep-bred resentment against any political policy labeled "Republican."

FEEDING THE POOR AT NEW ORLEANS.

CULVER SERVICE.

"CARPET-BAGGERS," "SCALAWAGS," AND A SOUTHERN LEGISLATURE

The end of the war brought an influx of poor Northerners to the South. They came carrying in carpet-bags all their possessions. Hence the term of derision. Many of the Negroes, who had suddenly gained the vote by reason of the hasty passage of the Fourteenth and Fifteenth amendments, fell easily under the influence of the worst "carpet-baggers," and the ensuing corruption, especially in the legislatures, was worse than anything the country experienced before or since. The "scalawags" were poor whites who saw in reconstruction a chance to better themselves and began to run for political office on the Republican ticket.

Plan of the Contemplated Murder of John Campbell.

(Entered according to Act of Congress, September, 1871, by T. B. Stamph.)

THE scene which furnishes the subject of the above engraving, was witnessed at a place known as Big Poplar, Moore county, North Carolina, on the night of the 19th of August. A man named John Campbell, a worthy resident of that locality, by his strict and earnest devotion to the cause of the Republican party, placed himself under the ban of the "White Brotherhood." He had been adjudged guilty at one of their many secret meetings of this, to their opinion, crime, and sentenced to be hung. Of course the victim was unconscious of the fate in store for him, and was quietly resting in his home when the murderous band of Ku-Klux, who had been charged with the duty of dispatching him, surrounded the house, captured their inoffensive and unsuspecting prey, secured his own wagon, then in solemn procession marched to an adjoining wood where the hellish deed was to be consummated. But an agent for their destruction was there, of which they little dreamed. Under one of the disguises strode the stalwart figure of a faithful agent of the Government, in the per-

son of Captain Joseph G. Hester, one of the oft-tried employees of the United States secret service. He had his arrangements made, as will be subsequently shown in the article, and unless some unforeseen accident occurred the captive then being led to his death would soon be free.

Arrived at the wood Campbell was taken from the wagon, and a half circle formed of the murderous brotherhood; the rope was produced, the hangman's noose placed over the head of the intended martyr, who, trembling with fear, was made to kneel before the assassinating band, thirsting for his blood, while the dread sentence of death was pronounced upon him. This scene of terror is faithfully depicted by our artist. With cowled head the Ku-Klux stand, their hands grasping the cord with which they expected soon to swing their victim into eternity. The sentence was pronounced, a movement was made to proceed with the execution, when suddenly Hester gave the signal he had previously arranged. Instantly the fiendish gang were surrounded with armed men, the rope

matched from the neck of the liberated captive, the disguises stripped from his captors; strong hands seized theirs, and the timely handcuff made to perform its functions.

The prisoners were marched to Raleigh, where Capt. Hester, with a desire that the people at large may know, without actual inspection, what a Ku Klux tribunal looks like, formed the group as it was formed in the woods, photographed it, and from the copy forwarded by him to the Secretary of War we have caused to be made a faithful fac simile in wood, which is presented to our readers. The names of some of the party engaged in this operation are as follows: Wm. W. Wicker, Jesse Bryan, J. W. Gaster, Wm. J. Bryan, R. W. Bryan and D. McIver, all of Moore county.

Bryan and Wicker, who are charged with the murder of Murchison McLane, were committed to jail to await an examination which is postponed two weeks for want of witness. The other four were allowed to give bail in the sum of $2,000 each for their appearance

at the September term of the United States Circuit Court.

John Gaster turned State's evidence, and his developments will reveal a state of affairs which will startle the public, and implicate parties little suspected.

Of course Hester's part in the capture narrated could not be kept secret, and the Democratic press in some portions of the State opened up against them their vials of wrath. We quote from the Fayetteville Eagle the manner in which the editor proposes to get clear of this faithful ally of the Government:

"Hester and other suspicious characters are prowling around in the country as secret detectives, really secret agents of the Radical officials, to keep up political hate and strife for profit to that party and its leaders. We hope our citizens will shoot down, on sight, any strangers caught in mischief while sneaking stealthily about our houses. A legitimate and well-meaning Government employee should be respected and assisted; but an assassin and incendiary, and a base tool for low-lived treachery and oppression, should not be allowed to carry out his nefarious purposes."

THE KU KLUX KLAN

Reconstruction as dictated by Congress led to inevitable violence. The South, determined to keep the freedmen peaceable and their white leaders in check, organized the Ku Klux Klan. First, its members resorted only to ghostly visits, then came whippings, tar, and feathers, and finally death. In 1871 Congress gave the President the right to suppress the organization, and the South, having had enough of violence, disbanded it. From a practical point of view, it had served its purpose.

236

JOHNSON'S IMPEACHMENT TRIAL

Conflict between the President and the radicals over reconstruction policies at last reached such a state that the Senate made an attempt to impeach him. He was uncouth, at least on one occasion under the influence of liquor, and rash in his statements. These, however, were not crimes. As the trial progressed, the nation and some few in Congress relented. On May 16, 1867, the vote was taken in breathless anticipation. Johnson held his office by one vote. The radicals were defeated. The country returned to sanity.

237

FROM "FRANK LESLIE'S ILLUSTRATED NEWSPAPER" FOR SEPTEMBER 3, 1864.

MAXIMILIAN'S RECEPTION AT MEXICO CITY

Ferdinand Maximilian's attempt to establish himself as emperor of Mexico was halted in 1865 when, the coming of peace having left the United States with a large army still mobilized, the federal government demanded that the French troops, which had subdued Mexico from 1861 on, be withdrawn. Napoleon acceded, but Maximilian stuck to his post. Surrounded by corruption he was betrayed at Querétaro, in 1867, captured by the Mexicans and, despite our pleas and those of others, shot.

238

PURCHASE OF ALASKA: NEW ARCHANGEL IN 1867

In both the Maximilian affair and the securing of Alaska in 1867, Seward, Johnson's Secretary of State, showed himself adept at foreign affairs. Alaska's fur trade and fishing industry were valuable, but Russia found it too remote to govern well, and fearing it might be seized by England, asked whether the United States was interested in purchasing the territory. The suggestion was quickly accepted. In one evening a price of $7,000,000 was agreed on, and a treaty drawn before either of the parties had a chance to change their minds. In the text accompanying the above illustration in *Harper's Weekly* the editors of that magazine were skeptical of the bargain that had been made. Admitting that the new possessions were large, they said, "their value is another question."

FROM "HARPER'S WEEKLY" FOR MAY 4, 1867.

239

BUILDING THE TRANSCONTINENTAL RAILROAD: DRIVING THE GOLDEN SPIKE

The linking of East and West by rail was the climax of one of the most colorful stories of American commercial enterprise. Although planned before the Civil War, the transcontinental railroad was not completed till several years afterward. Aided by government funds, the Union Pacific built westward and the Central Pacific eastward. The frantic race between the two was for the valuable land grants, as well as the subsidies, that went with each mile of new track. At Promontory Point, Utah, on May 10, 1869, a golden spike was driven into the last tie. The Central Pacific was said to have won by a small margin.

THE NEW YORK STOCK EXCHANGE ON "BLACK FRIDAY"

The panic of September 24, 1869, came as the result of an attempt by Jay Gould and James Fisk, Jr., to corner the country's gold supply. Gould had wormed his way into the good graces of President Grant and made him an unwitting partner to the manipulation. Gold rose from 132 to 162. During the price rise Gould sold not only to the public but to Fisk. When the government broke the corner by selling gold, Gould was safely out of the market with a handsome profit, Fisk was ruined, and Grant discredited.

THE CHICAGO FIRE

The great Chicago fire began on October 8, 1871. The conflagration, said to have started in a stable where a cow kicked over a lighted lamp, burned for three days, in some places reached the edge of the prairie itself, consumed three and a half square miles of city buildings, snuffed out two hundred and fifty lives, and caused a loss of about $200,000,000. It was not without its benefits to the future citizens of Chicago, however, for the people of the city rapidly rebuilt it along finer and more splendid lines.

THE GREAT TIDE OF IMMIGRATION: EMBARKATION FOR NEW YORK

A great period of prosperity was attained throughout the country, except in the ruined South, from 1865 to 1873. The railroad projects, followed by agricultural expansion in the West, and many new enterprises which were now beginning, created a demand for cheap labor. It was supplied from abroad. Hundreds of thousands of immigrants were soon swarming into our ports, many of them being unsuited to life in the new country. This was the beginning of the long period in which the United States became the "melting pot" of the world.

FROM "HARPER'S WEEKLY" FOR OCTOBER 11, 1873.

PANIC OF 1873: OFFICES OF JAY COOKE & CO.

Over-expansion brought its consequences in September, 1873. The banking firm of Jay Cooke & Co. had financed the building of the Northern Pacific. At about the same time there was a sharp panic in Vienna, Austria, and Europe, alarmed, ceased buying American bonds. Gradually it became apparent that Cooke could not market the Northern Pacific securities. The firm's admission of insolvency on the 18th started a bank run, and this uncertainty eventually spreading to the entire business structure of the nation, began a long period of "hard times."

244

RISE OF THE TEMPERANCE CRUSADE

A temperance movement grew rapidly in the 1870's and 1880's. Although there had been agitation against strong drink for years, it was not till 1874 that the National Woman's Christian Temperance Union was founded. Frances Willard became the moving spirit in the organization. Although this picture shows the temperance advocates in a pacific mood, on many occasions destruction of all movable furnishings marked their visits to a saloon.

FROM "THE DAILY GRAPHIC" FOR MARCH 5, 1874.

THE BELKNAP SCANDAL AND GRANT'S POLITICAL MISTAKES

Although honest himself, Grant had an easy toleration of corruption in others, and his two terms marked the heyday of the spoilsman. Following the Gould-Fisk speculation came the Credit Mobilier frauds, the Whisky Ring, and the Belknap scandal in 1876, in which it was said that Belknap, Grant's Secretary of War, accepted a bribe to keep an Indian agent in office. It was inevitable that the corrupt and often illicit, but very profitable, trade with the Indians in the West should bring corruption to high places. With none of these scandals was Grant directly involved, but his friends and advisers were, and his reputation suffered accordingly.

FROM A CARTOON BY THOMAS NAST IN "HARPER'S WEEKLY" FOR MARCH 25, 1876.

246

THE DISPUTED ELECTION OF 1876: THE COMMISSION IN SESSION

The Presidential election of 1876 resulted in a political dispute of serious proportions. Rutherford B. Hayes, Republican, had 184 undisputed votes, Samuel J. Tilden, Democrat, 165, with twenty from South Carolina, Louisiana, Florida, and Oregon, in dispute. Tilden needed them all to be elected. Eventually an electoral commission of fifteen men was appointed by Congress to decide the issue. On this there were eight Republicans and seven Democrats. Its decision was along strictly party lines, and Hayes became President.

247

CUSTER MASSACRE: CUSTER RAIDS AN INDIAN CAMP

The Sioux War of 1876 was the last serious attempt of the Indian to hold by arms some of the land to which he had been born. Joining with the Cheyennes, the Sioux, under their able leader Sitting Bull, raised a powerful force of some six thousand braves. In late June they trapped General G.A. Custer and six hundred men near the junction of the Big Horn and the Little Big Horn rivers in South Dakota. Not a soldier in Custer's party escaped. The slaughter was probably as ruthless as the Army's methods had been in attacking Indian villages.

248

THE CENTENNIAL EXPOSITION: OPENING DAY

The Centennial Exposition held in Philadelphia in 1876 celebrated the one hundredth anniversary of American independence. It was the world's outstanding affair of that character held up to that time. Its educational and cultural advantages were great, for foreign and domestic contacts were then vastly less than today. Every important foreign country participated and Americans were thrown into touch with old-world products and culture as never before. Directly and indirectly, it had a material influence on international trade.

FROM "HARPER'S WEEKLY" FOR MAY 27, 1876.

THE CORLISS STEAM ENGINE AT THE CENTENNIAL

One of the high spots of the Exposition was the starting of the great Corliss steam engine, the wonder of the day, which turned the machinery in Machinery Hall. Dom Pedro, the emperor of Brazil, accompanied by President Grant, turned on the power which put the huge machine in motion. It was purchased by the Pullman Company following the close of the Exposition and for many years ran in its plant at Chicago.

250

BELL DEMONSTRATES THE TELEPHONE AT SALEM

Included in an educational exhibit from Massachusetts at the Centennial Exposition was a device destined to revolutionize sound transmission. It had been sent there by a young Scotsman named Alexander Graham Bell. It attracted little attention until, in the following year, a public exhibition of the "telephone" was given at Salem, Massachusetts. To the amazement of those present, a spoken message was successfully transmitted from that city to the office of a Boston newspaper.

FROM "FRANK LESLIE'S ILLUSTRATED NEWSPAPER" FOR MARCH 31, 1877.

THE ELECTRIC LIGHT

Many had experimented with electric lighting before Thomas A. Edison
put in circuit the first commercially successful lamp on October 21, 1879.
When the New York papers announced that Edison was lighting the streets
of Menlo Park, New Jersey, with his new lamp, the Pennsylvania Railroad
installed special trains to accommodate those who came to see the marvel.
The picture shows New York, near the Fifth Avenue Hotel, when the city
was illuminated by Brush arc lamps.

RIOTS AGAINST THE CHINESE, AND EXCLUSION

The presence of many Chinese in the Far West did not cause much opposition until white laborers, pouring in with the coming of the transcontinental railroads, complained because the Chinese worked long hours for little pay. Serious riots against them took place in many cities, such as the one shown below in Denver in 1880. Hayes finally negotiated a treaty with China which for ten years excluded Chinese laborers. Later, this treaty was extended indefinitely. It was always difficult to enforce, due to smuggling.

FROM "FRANK LESLIE'S ILLUSTRATED NEWSPAPER" FOR NOVEMBER 20, 1880.

253

FROM "FRANK LESLIE'S ILLUSTRATED NEWSPAPER" FOR JANUARY 8, 1881.

SPECIE PAYMENT AND THE PROSPEROUS YEARS

Specie payment was not resumed by the United States until 1879. The question then was, could it be maintained? Two fortuitous events made this possible, first, a general failure of European crops causing a demand for our farm supplies; second, the failure of the cotton crop in India. Both helped turn the balance of trade in our favor and our gold remained with us. The picture, showing a levee in New Orleans in 1881, was entitled "The Business Boom in the South," at the time of its publication. Prosperity was nation-wide in the years 1879 to 1881.

GARFIELD'S ASSASSINATION: TRIAL OF GUITEAU

On July 2, 1881, while on his way to attend the Commencement exercises at Williams College, James A. Garfield, who had been in office but four months, was approached in the Washington railway station by a disappointed office seeker named Charles J. Guiteau, who shot him. He died on September 19th. During those weeks in which he lay suffering, much of the political feeling against him, due to his countenancing of some of the practices of the spoilsmen, disappeared. Guiteau, who was an obscure Chicago lawyer of French-Canadian descent, was tried and convicted in Washington, where he was hanged on June 30, 1882.

FROM "FRANK LESLIE'S ILLUSTRATED NEWSPAPER" FOR DECEMBER 3, 1881.

255

THE OPENING OF THE BROOKLYN BRIDGE

One of the great engineering feats of the late 19th century was the building of the Brooklyn Bridge. The success of the venture was, in large measure, due to the Roebling brothers who made the gigantic cables that held up the roadway. One of them died in the construction work. Some time after it was opened in 1883 someone on the span suddenly shouted that it was falling and several persons were killed in the wild panic that followed.

CIVIL SERVICE REFORM

The period from 1881 to 1893 was marked by political and economic reform. One of the first things accomplished was the Civil Service Act of 1883. At last, in the face of an overwhelming public feeling against the spoils system, Congress gave way. Since 1883 successive Presidents have perfected and enlarged the system. Under Harrison, Theodore Roosevelt made the service a powerful agent for good. Congress feared him, the spoilsmen hated him, but the people trusted his judgment. The picture, "The Franking Abuse," shows bags of free mail leaving Washington. The Post Office was the prey for the spoilsmen and was soon affected for the better by the Civil Service reforms.

FROM A CARTOON IN "PUCK" BY F. OPPER.

257

"RUM, ROMANISM, AND REBELLION"

In 1884 the statement of one of James G. Blaine's admirers, a New York divine, to the effect that he and his friends would not vote for the party of "Rum, Romanism, and Rebellion," very likely caused his defeat. Blaine was at the reception when these words were spoken and in replying to the minister's speech, he took no notice of the slight to the Catholic church. The election hung on the outcome in New York which went Democratic by 1149 votes. With the result so close, it is probable that the statement turned the balance for Grover Cleveland, the Democratic candidate. The picture shows the reception at which the damaging statement was made.

FROM "HARPER'S WEEKLY" FOR MAY 15, 1886.

THE HAYMARKET RIOTS

As the nation's industrial workers increased in numbers, organized labor under the banner of the Knights of Labor grew in power. Within the organization were many advocates of direct action and, at an anarchists' meeting in Haymarket Square, Chicago, in 1886, a bomb was thrown killing seven people. Eight anarchists were arrested. The country was vastly excited at this appearance of violence, and of the eight, four were hung, one committed suicide, and two received life sentences. The thrower of the bomb was never identified. People, generally, approved the sentences, although many have always maintained that the men were the victims of public hysteria and a prejudiced judge, and were given a trial that was irregular in many respects.

FROM "HARPER'S WEEKLY" FOR JULY 25, 1868.

FORMATION OF THE AMERICAN FEDERATION OF LABOR

The American Federation of Labor was organized under that name in 1886 while public reaction against the Knights was still strong. It held that workers in each trade should organize in their own interests, a system suited to the nature of American industry. Its growth was remarkable. Its earliest activities were devoted to securing shorter working hours. The picture shows New England mill workers in 1868 when twelve-hour shifts, employing women and children, were not uncommon. It was against such conditions that first the Knights and then the American Federation of Labor turned their efforts.

RAILROAD BUILDING AND CONSOLIDATION: A CHICAGO RAILWAY STATION

The period from 1850 on was first one of great railway construction, interrupted by the Civil War and the panics of 1857 and 1873, and then one of railway consolidation. In this era grew the nuclei of the New York Central, the Pennsylvania, and the Baltimore & Ohio systems. While consolidation went on, new tracks were being laid, especially in the west on the Central Pacific, the Union Pacific, the Northern Pacific, the Southern Pacific, the Santa Fé, and the Great Northern lines. From all this activity Chicago, as a junction point, benefited and its station platforms were the meeting points of the East and West.

261

THE INTERSTATE COMMERCE COMMISSION ACT

Railroad consolidation brought evils in its wake. Public distrust of the roads led to the formation of the Granges in the West which, in their turn, hastened the coming of the first Interstate Commerce Commission Act in 1887. This act gave the commission no jurisdiction over rates and no power to enforce its decisions. Hence freight re- bates to favored shippers and discrimination against other shippers and shipping points went on as before, until after the turn of the century. The arm stretching from the White House, in the cartoon, is Cleveland's, under whose administration the I. C. C. Act was passed.

262

"HARPER'S WEEKLY" FOR JULY 27, 1889.

THE McKINLEY TARIFF: STEAMER DAY IN NEW YORK

A tariff was the first legislative act passed by the United States. That was in 1789. Ever since, protection has been a political battleground. The rise of American industry, and, to some degree, the need for revenue, spurred the tariff acts of the eighties and nineties. The McKinley Tariff of 1890 advanced rates somewhat. An attempt was made to embody in this bill the principle of reciprocity, but, as it was finally passed, it acted more as a club by which we were able to get trade concessions, especially from the South American countries. In 1894 the Wilson Bill brought reductions, but in 1897 the Dingley Bill raised the wall again. Capital and labor being in agreement on the subject of protection, this bill remained until 1909.

THE JOHNSTOWN FLOOD

Johnstown, Pennsylvania, was on May 31, 1889, the scene of one of the greatest disasters in American history. An abandoned reservoir, about twelve miles above the city, gave way and a huge mass of water tore down the valley of the Conemaugh River. The flood swept away the city and with it about three thousand lives. Some said that the flood was caused by excessive lumbering in the section which had denuded the surrounding hills, changing the natural drainage.

FROM "HARPER'S WEEKLY" FOR JUNE 15, 1889.

SHERMAN ANTI-TRUST ACT

This period was also one of great combinations in the industrial field. John D. Rockefeller first proved it possible to monopolize not only a public service but the manufacture of an article, with the formation of the Standard Oil Trust. Small business and the general public were instinctively against the trust and it became a political issue in 1888. In 1890 was passed the Sherman Anti-Trust Law. It declared illegal contracts to create monopolies in restraint of trade. It made no distinction between good and bad combinations, and later, changes became necessary in the anti-trust laws.

FROM A CARTOON BY W. A. ROGERS IN "HARPER'S WEEKLY" FOR DECEMBER 3, 1887.

FROM A CARTOON BY J. KEPPLER IN "PUCK" FOR FEBRUARY 6, 1889.

THE SAMOAN INCIDENT

The Samoan Islands in the Pacific became the subject of a controversy in 1889 among the United States, Great Britain, and Germany. War ships were anchored off the islands and a conflict seemed imminent when on March 16th a hurricane destroyed all but one of the vessels. A joint protectorate was then formed from which Great Britain later withdrew, the United States taking the island of Tutuila, and Germany the rest. During the incident there was hard feeling among the three nations, especially between the United States and Germany. In the World War, Germany lost her portion.

266

THE MAFIA INCIDENT: MURDER OF THE ITALIANS

On March 15, 1891, a mob in New Orleans broke open a prison where several Italians, suspected of being connected with the Mafia Society, a well-known Italian organization, and implicated in the murder of the city's chief of police, were detained. Nine were shot down. Washington could not grant the satisfaction Italy demanded because no federal law had been violated and Italy withdrew her representative. Most of the victims were American citizens and with this discovery Italy relented and an incident, for a moment dangerous, passed over.

FROM "HARPER'S WEEKLY" FOR MARCH 28, 1891.

FROM "FRANK LESLIE'S WEEKLY" FOR APRIL 7, 1892.

FUR SEAL CONTROVERSY: SLAUGHTER OF THE SEALS

During President Harrison's administration the slaughter of the fur seals in Bering Sea was widely criticized. The United States claimed that its ownership of the Pribiloff Islands gave it the right to control sealing in the whole of the Bering Sea and proceeded to arrest persons taking seals contrary to its regulations. Great Britain vigorously protested. Public opinion in both countries was against violence and this forced a settlement in 1893. The two countries thereafter jointly regulated the industry.

THE HOMESTEAD STRIKE: SURRENDER OF THE PINKERTON MEN

Continuing industrial growth during the prosperous years after 1886 brought a corresponding increase in the power of organized labor which made possible the great strike at Homestead, Pennsylvania, in 1892, against the Carnegie Steel Company. In a battle between the workers and about two hundred detectives of the Pinkerton agency, seven were killed. Soldiers were called to keep order and the trouble died down. The conflict was won by the company and it was the last serious effort of the steel workers for a quarter of a century.

FROM "HARPER'S WEEKLY" FOR JULY 16, 1892.

THE PANIC OF 1893: THE STOCK EXCHANGE ON AUGUST 12

The panic of 1893 started when Europe began selling American securities and withdrawing gold. Our ability to maintain specie payment was threatened. Cleveland feared the public would begin hoarding gold. Business distress rapidly became widespread. When the Silver Purchase Law of 1890 was repealed in 1893, the West and the South felt that they had been betrayed by Cleveland. The gold-silver controversy now became more bitter than ever. The picture illustrates one of the flurries on the Stock Exchange during the panic.

270

THE PULLMAN STRIKE: TROOPS GUARDING MEAT TRAINS

Following the panic of 1893 came reduction in wages, and in the Pullman company's works near Chicago a great strike ensued. Governor Altgeld, sympathetic to labor, refused to call out the militia and eventually Cleveland sent federal troops to release the tie-up of trains. After the strike the public showed plainly that it was irked by both capital and labor for causing costly strikes, the expenses for which came out of the nation's pocket.

FROM "HARPER'S WEEKLY" FOR JULY 28, 1894.

COXEY'S ARMY

FROM "HARPER'S WEEKLY" FOR MAY 12, 1894.

Numerous panaceas were proposed to relieve distress following the panic of 1893. One of these, made by Jacob S. Coxey, was to issue $500,000,000 in currency and with it pay for road construction. It would, he said, relieve unemployment, give the nation good roads, and allow distressed debtors to pay off their obligations. The "General," in a novel publicity stunt, gathered about one hundred men and started a march on Washington. On May 1, 1894, at the Capitol, the leaders were arrested for trespassing on the grass.

272

THE WORLD'S FAIR OF 1893

While the country was in the midst of the depression of 1893 there was held at Chicago the Columbian Exposition, popularly called the World's Fair, to celebrate the 400th anniversary of the landing of Columbus. Beautifully laid out on the shore of Lake Michigan, the principal buildings were of unusual architectural beauty. The possibilities of electrical illumination had only recently been fully realized. To many, the exposition, in addition to being a remarkable industrial exhibit was, at night, fairyland realized.

FROM A DRAWING BY THULSTRUP IN "HARPER'S WEEKLY."

273

RISE OF THE NAVY: THE "WHITE SQUADRON"

The Act of 1883 marks the beginning of the rise of the American Navy to first-rank power. The picture shows the so-called White Squadron of the resuscitated fleet in 1889. The presence of the masts is accounted for by the fact that the debate over sails continued almost to 1900.

The renaissance was given enormous impetus by Admiral Alfred T. Mahan who, in his able and widely read books, showed for the first time the great importance of sea power as a decisive factor in history.

274

BRYAN AND 16 TO 1

In 1896 bimetalism and the proposal to establish silver at a ratio of 16 to 1 to gold was the paramount issue, with the young Democrats of the South and West in open revolt against their party. All they needed was a leader. They found and acclaimed him in William Jennings Bryan who, at the Democratic Convention in a famous speech cried out, "You shall not press down upon the brow of labor this crown of thorns; you shall not crucify mankind upon a cross of gold." He won the nomination.

FROM "HARPER'S WEEKLY" FOR AUGUST 29, 1896.

McKINLEY AND GOLD: A FRONT–PORCH SPEECH

The millionaire politician from Cleveland, Marcus A. Hanna, was responsible for securing the Republican nomination for William McKinley on a gold standard platform. It was a violent campaign with Bryan going to the people in a nationwide tour, a method of vote-getting which was to become the accepted thing in subsequent Presidential contests. Bryan was defeated but not subdued. He was to remain the leader of the Democratic party for many years. The picture shows McKinley receiving a delegation on his front porch, a method of campaigning in sharp contrast to that of Bryan.

276

THE KLONDIKE GOLD RUSH OF 1896

In the midst of the gold-silver campaign sensational deposits of the yellow metal were discovered in the Klondike region of western Canada in August, 1896. Then started the most picturesque gold rush in all history. This unusual photograph of the actual rush shows hundreds of gold seekers camped in the snow while others push on over rugged Chilkoot Pass. Thirty thousand from all parts of the country joined in the frantic search for the yellow metal.

277

FROM "HARPER'S WEEKLY" FOR AUGUST 13, 1898.

HAWAII ANNEXED: THE PROCLAMATION READ IN HONOLULU

In 1882 the reigning king of Hawaii proclaimed a constitution granting suffrage to whites as well as to natives. Its repeal in 1893 by Queen Liliuokalani was followed by a revolution. The queen was deposed and an invitation extended to the United States for annexation. No action to that end was taken until 1898 when, following the Spanish-American War, the desirability of an American mid-Pacific naval base became apparent and Hawaii was annexed as a territory.

278

PILGRIMS OF THE PLAINS

The Civil War only checked the westward flow of our civilization. After the war this increased greatly, augmented by the flood of immigration from Europe. For a time this wave of settlement jumped over the vast plains between the Mississippi and the Rockies, first, because scanty rainfall made farming there none too easy, and second, because in that section the Indian was still at large, resolved to make a last stand against civilization.

MINING IN THE WEST: A STREET IN LEADVILLE

The activities of prospectors continued to be a powerful influence in opening certain parts of the West. In 1859 the famous Comstock Lode was discovered in Nevada. The wealth of this bonanza mine was enormous and for a time it produced half of the silver mined in the United States. By 1886 most of its mines were abandoned and it had given way to the Leadville district in Colorado which in one year yielded $11,000,000 worth of the white metal.

THE COUNTRY STORE

The country store filled a place in American life so long as the old farm existed. The coming of the railroad, more efficient farm machinery and, much later, the automobile, made an end of the general store as a universal American institution. Above all, the store was a meeting place. Round its pot-bellied stove, glowing-red on winter days, and its coal scuttle which served as a spittoon, gossip, news, politics, and the crops were discussed.

© CURTIS PUBLISHING COMPANY

281

THE COMMON SCHOOL

The great desire of the late 19th century farmer was to give his children the education that had been denied him in the pioneer days. Almost every district in the West saw that it had its tiny school building. To this boys and girls came, often over many miles of rough roads or no roads at all, to be given the bare fundamentals of an education. All ages, from toddlers up to eighteen and twenty, were taught in one room. In such schools many children, some of them destined to become the best-known men and women in the country, received their only schooling.

282

MACHINERY ON THE FARM

Machinery made it possible to put great areas of the West under successful cultivation. Almost every decade from the time of the first McCormick reaper witnessed improvements in the art of husbandry. Not the least of these was the development of the harvesting and threshing combine in the 1880's. The picture shows farm hands and machinery ready to move on in the wheat section of the northwest. The traveling harvest hand was a type of labor unknown before the Civil War.

FROM "HARPER'S WEEKLY" FOR DECEMBER 13, 1890.

FROM "HARPER'S WEEKLY" FOR OCTOBER 17, 1868.

THE COUNTRY CHURCH

The years after the Civil War were those in which the churches of America came to maturity. While the older and stronger organizations were increasing their memberships, a great many smaller sects also came into prominence. The most influential factor in the religious life of the rural community remained the country church where, in horse and buggy, came the townspeople and the country folk dressed in their Sunday best to worship and meet their friends and neighbors.

284

THE COUNTY FAIR

Unlike the first fairs held in this country, which were for the sale and exchange of goods, county fairs were held to exhibit the finest products of the farm. Prizes were offered for everything from pies to bulls and the competition was keen. Horse races, side shows, barkers, and all the rest, were added to make the fair more exciting. Eventually the idea was enlarged to embrace the state and these widened the farmer's contacts with the outside world.

W. J. Palmer Sc.

FROM "HARPER'S WEEKLY" FOR SEPTEMBER 11, 1875.

THE COW COUNTRY AND THE COWBOY

The first settlers after the pioneers ignored the so-called "American desert," but once the possibilities of ranching had been proved the great cow country sprang into existence from Texas northward and from the Missouri River to the Rockies. Its most colorful character was the cowboy, the last of the American frontier types. With all his faults the cowboy developed a code that demanded honest and courageous living in order to survive, beset as he was by Indians, horse thieves, and unscrupulous adventurers.

SINKING OF THE "MAINE"

Spanish rule in Cuba, rightly or wrongly, stirred in Americans the desire to see that country free. A financial interest in the island, which was no larger than Spain's, also influenced our attitude. The sinking of the battleship *Maine* in Havana harbor on February 15, 1898, with a loss of two hundred and sixty men, raised a storm that could not be resisted, despite McKinley's efforts to keep peace. The people of the United States wanted war, and an end of Spanish rule in the western world.

BATTLE OF MANILA BAY

The military part of the war divides into two sections. The first of these was against Spain's possessions in the Pacific. Admiral George Dewey met part of the enemy's fleet at Manila Bay in the Philippine Islands on May 1, 1898, and completely destroyed it. He could do nothing further until August 13, when, a land force having been sent him, he occupied the city of Manila. Thus did we come to have a hand in the international problems of the Pacific.

TROOPS LANDING IN CUBA

The second half of the war was in Cuba. The finest vessels in the Spanish fleet under Admiral Cervera had gone to Santiago, whence he intended to sail and then menace the Atlantic ports. Before he could escape, however, he was bottled up by the American navy under Commodore Winfield S. Schley and later under Admiral William T. Sampson. The best known incident of the blockade was the exploit of Lieutenant Richard P. Hobson and six men in sinking the *Merrimac* in the harbor's channel. They volunteered, thinking death almost a certainty, but they escaped and became national heroes. Again nothing could be done before there was a land force, and Sampson requested troops. On June 22d they began to come ashore under General William R. Shafter. They included the famous Rough Riders (without horses) under Leonard Wood, with Theodore Roosevelt second-in-command.

TROOPS ENTRENCHED AT SAN JUAN HILL

On July first came the attack on the city of Santiago. The first advance on the outlying village of El Caney was delayed by a brave but greatly outnumbered Spanish force. Finally it was successful. Meanwhile the second half of the attack on San Juan Hill had likewise been delayed by stubborn opposition. Eventually, without orders, the Americans charged and annihilated the tiny band of defenders. The city itself did not surrender until July 17th when, Cervera's fleet having been destroyed, its doom became inevitable.

BATTLE OF SANTIAGO

On July 3rd, Cervera, not willing to surrender his fleet without a battle, decided to run for it. Bravely he led the procession out of Santiago harbor. Once in the open, instead of scattering, the Spanish ships gave battle, but either their powder was poor or their aim was bad, and it soon became clear that the struggle was an unequal one. Within four hours Cervera lost every one of his ships. Throughout the war the navy showed to better advantage than the land forces, due to the fact that the latter were poorly equipped.

291

THE "OPEN DOOR" POLICY: THE OLD SHANGHAI BUND

John Hay, Secretary of State under McKinley, won what was apparently a great diplomatic victory at a time when the European Powers were establishing themselves in vast zones "leased" from the helpless government of China and threatening exclusion of American trade. In September, 1899, Secretary Hay secured the consent of the powers to refrain from interference with Chinese customs collections at any of the twenty-two treaty ports, and to open their "spheres of influence" to other nations. Unfortunately, the beneficial effects anticipated for the "open door" policy proved to be in some degree illusory.

THE BOXER OUTBREAK: THE AMERICAN REFUGE

Early in 1900, foreign residents in China found themselves in the midst of a rebellion sponsored by a secret society known as "The Boxers", with the purpose of expelling all outsiders from Chinese soil. Missionaries were murdered, while at Pekin the inmates of the legations defended themselves for weeks in enclosures such as that shown above. Troops of several nations landed, defeated the Chinese, and rescued the besieged legations. The powers imposed territorial and financial indemnities on China, the United States eventually returning its share. American moderation in the matter did much to promote friendly relations with the Chinese.

© C. A. KILLIE.

293

NORTHERN PACIFIC PANIC

An effort of the Harriman interests to secure control of Northern Pacific securities resulted in a clash with the Hill-Morgan financial group. The financial battle culminated in the panic of May 9, 1901, when Northern Pacific common soared to $1000 on the Stock Exchange. Harriman secured a majority interest in the road, but control of the common was retained by Hill and the matter was settled by formation of the Northern Securities Company, later dissolved by the Supreme Court.

FROM THE "NEW YORK HERALD," MAY 9, 1901.

BEGINNING OF THE MOVIES

The above scene is from the first motion picture to embody a plot, "The Great Train Robbery," an adaptation of fiction to the screen by one of Thomas A. Edison's staff. It was a momentous day for America when, in 1903, this primitive forerunner of today's "epics" was shown. It was the injection of a story which started the public flocking to early theaters, known as "nickelodeons" because of the price of admission. The story-picture created a great new industry and exerted a deep influence on civilization, with the future still undefined.

FORMATION OF THE I. W. W.

Regarding Socialist doctrines as too peaceful, a group of advocates of "direct action" organized the Industrial Workers of the World in Chicago in 1905. For years the extreme "left-wingers" had been active in an unorganized way, and had engaged in riots such as the one shown below in Tompkins Square, New York, in the middle seventies. The new organization was promptly repudiated by the Socialists and the labor unions. The World War brought about the decline of the movement.

FROM "FRANK LESLIE'S ILLUSTRATED NEWSPAPER" FOR JANUARY 31, 1874.

THE RISE OF LABOR: SAMUEL GOMPERS

Organized labor's growth to national influence occurred during the early nineteen-hundreds under the adroit leadership of Samuel Gompers, a former London cigar-maker's apprentice. Early reforms included the eight-hour law for Government workers, the ten-hour law for street railway employees. The designation of the first Monday in September as "Labor Day," a national holiday, was another of Gompers' achievements. Such were his abilities, that during the years of his presidency, 1882–1924 (with the exception of one year), the American Federation of Labor became a potent factor in the economic, industrial, and political life of the country.

RAILROAD REGULATION: THE HEPBURN ACT

Passage of the Hepburn Act, June 29, 1906, by Congress imposed severe penalties on railroad rebating and unjust discrimination against shippers. The Interstate Commerce Commission was empowered to prescribe rates, subject to court review, and schedules of all tariffs were required to be filed with that body, which was also authorized to prescribe a uniform method of keeping accounts of the common carriers. Issuance of free passes was restricted to families of employees of the transportation companies. Express companies, sleeping-car companies, and oil pipe lines were also brought under the I. C. C. The picture shows the great freight yards of the Illinois Central in Chicago.

FOOD AND DRUG REGULATION AND INSPECTION

By the dawn of the Twentieth Century, adulteration of food articles, medicines and packing products had become so widespread as to constitute a national abuse. In 1906, Congress enacted legislation to cover interstate commerce in such commodities, prohibiting the manufacture and sale of those containing harmful substances, and compelling truthful labeling. On the same day that the Pure Food and Drugs Act was passed, Congress also placed the slaughtering and preparation of meats to be shipped over state lines subject to inspection by the Department of Agriculture. The picture shows part of the great stockyards of the meat packers, Armour & Co., in Chicago.

THE PANAMA CANAL

Defeated by yellow fever and malaria, a French company had abandoned construction of an inter-ocean canal across the Isthmus of Panama in 1889. With establishment of the Republic of Panama, the United States took up the work where the French left off. Sanitary measures inaugurated by Dr. William C. Gorgas ended the fever menace and saved thousands of workers' lives. The entire nation watched with pride the progress of the Army construction work. On August 15, 1914, the canal was opened to traffic of all nations. The photograph shows work on the Culebra Cut in 1908.

BY HINE FROM EWING GALLOWAY.

IMMIGRATION REACHES ITS CREST

Immigration to the United States touched a high mark by June, 1907, with admission of almost 1,300,000 aliens for the fiscal year. A movement which had been in progress for many decades had culminated, bringing in its wake important social changes and serious domestic problems. Although the tide that had engulfed the country was to recede, it was not to be finally checked until after the war. Above is a pre-war scene at Ellis Island, debarkation point for immigrants in New York.

301

FROM THE "NEW YORK AMERICAN" FOR OCTOBER 23, 1907.

THE PANIC OF 1907

A ten-year period of overcapitalization ended in the panic of October 22, 1907, when gilt-edged securities took an abrupt downward plunge following the closing of the Knickerbocker Trust Co. Wall Street interests charged that the Roosevelt policy of strict enforcement of regulations governing corporations was the cause, and the President countered that infractions of the law by corporations, not enforcement, were responsible. It advertised, however, the failure of the Currency Act of 1900 to stabilize the currency. It was short-lived and never became widespread.

THE FLEET SAILS ROUND THE WORLD

Resentment at increased Japanese immigration to the Pacific coast reached a high-water mark, especially among the newspapers and the labor elements in the West, in 1908. Perhaps as a warning, and to give the world a demonstration of American naval strength, President Roosevelt sent a fleet of twenty-eight war-ships in December for a round-the-world voyage, which was completed in February, 1909, without accident. At every port of call, including Yokohama, the personnel were received with enthusiasm and a cordial welcome, the President terming them "heralds of peace." The picture shows the fleet at San Francisco.

COURTESY UNITED STATES NAVY DEPARTMENT.

ADVENT OF THE AUTOMOBILE

To derisive cries of "Get a Horse" and a popular song, "Get Out and Get Under," the horseless carriage began to appear more frequently on the nation's crude highways as 1908 approached. After the first wave of popular resentment, the future possibilities of this new means of travel were quickly recognized and a new industry sprang into being. The transformation worked on the social habits of the country is still going on. The little boy perched on the back of this early automobile is Clarence Chamberlin, later to be famous as a transatlantic flyer.

AMERICAN CONTROL WITHDRAWN FROM CUBA

The provision of an orderly government in Cuba was one of the major problems resulting from the Spanish-American War. Europe frankly doubted our pledge to turn the island over to its people once they were able to conduct their affairs as a nation. From 1899 to 1902, General Leonard Wood carried out the work of establishing the new government, including a system of public education. Major Walter Reed stamped out yellow fever with his experiments proving that the mosquito transmitted the disease. The first Cuban general election was held in February, 1902, and on May 20th General Wood turned over the government to President Tomas Estrada Palma. The United States intervened in Cuba in 1906 and also in 1912 and 1917 to restore order or prevent revolutions threatening foreign interests, and has occasionally landed Marines. For years our policy in the island was dictated by the so-called Platt Amendment of 1901 which gave us the right to intervene to preserve independence, order, republican government, and to see that Cuba discharged her obligations to other nations. One of the policies sponsored by Franklin Roosevelt was the repeal of the Platt Amendment. The picture shows the United States fleet in Havana harbor after the Spanish-American War.

EWING GALLOWAY.

UNDERWOOD & UNDERWOOD.

THE BRYAN–CHAMORRO TREATY WITH NICARAGUA

Toward the close of Taft's administration Nicaragua offered to sell the United States the exclusive right to build a canal through that country and to establish forts at each end in return for $3,000,000. When William Jennings Bryan became Secretary of State, he sought to amend the offer so as to make Nicaragua an American protectorate. The Senate at Washington refused to approve this, and the Bryan-Chamorro Treaty of 1916 was confined to the original terms of 1912. The picture shows Nicaraguan rebels fighting loyal troops near Nicaragua.

THE CAMPAIGN OF 1912: ROOSEVELT NOMINATED AT THE
BULL MOOSE CONVENTION

The national campaign of 1912, marked by bitter personalities, saw Theodore Roosevelt again a candidate, splitting the Republican ranks with his Progressive, or Bull Moose, party. Taft, candidate for re-election, ran a poor third in the voting, which placed Woodrow Wilson, scholarly Democratic reformer, in the White House. It was the first Democratic victory since Cleveland's election, and was aided by many erstwhile Republicans.

THE INCOME TAX AMENDMENT

The Underwood Tariff of 1913 embodied a tax on all incomes as a means of compensating for decreases in customs revenues provided by the act. The income tax idea was not new, having been used during the Civil War, although an attempt to impose one in 1895 was declared unconstitutional by a 5 to 4 Supreme Court decision. This led ultimately to the Sixteenth Amendment to the Constitution. With some lapses, the general trend of income-tax rates has been upward, some states even imposing levies of their own.

POPULAR ELECTION OF SENATORS

The framers of the Constitution provided that Senators should be elected by state legislatures. Attempts to change this were immediate, but always met with defeat despite House victories. In 1904 Oregon permitted voters to indicate their Senatorial choice on ballots, and the movement spread until enough states to ratify a constitutional amendment were following this example. The Senate yielded in 1911, and the amendment calling for direct popular election of its members was ratified by three-fourths of the states and proclaimed part of the Constitution on May 31, 1913. The picture shows Bryan signing the announcement of the Seventeenth Amendment.

THE FEDERAL RESERVE ACT

Growth of the currency and banking problem brought about the Federal Reserve Act of December 23, 1913, by which the country was divided into twelve districts with a member bank in a central city in each. All national banks were required to enter the reserve system, which provided for acceptance of approved "paper" in exchange for Federal Reserve notes whenever expansion of the currency is required by business conditions. Although advocates of the Act encountered widespread resistance, it has since proved its worth in coping with the ever-fluctuating business and financial conditions of the country. The picture shows, right, the Federal Reserve bank in New York.

310

THE OCCUPATION OF VERA CRUZ

In 1913, Victoriano Huerta was president of Mexico, his henchmen having murdered his predecessor. To combat the usurper, President Wilson raised the embargo on arms to revolutionists fighting the Huerta regime. In April, 1914, sailors from the U. S. S. *Dolphin*, landing at Tampico to buy gasoline, were arrested and detained by Huerta's officers, and the United States, obtaining their release, demanded a salute to our flag as formal apology. Huerta refused, and the battleships *Utah* and *Florida* shelled the arsenal at Vera Cruz and landed Marines who captured the city. Huerta eventually resigned and left Mexico. Above, transferring refugees from Vera Cruz to our warships.

THE PANAMA–PACIFIC INTERNATIONAL EXPOSITION

This exposition, held in San Francisco in 1915, celebrated the opening of the Panama Canal and the quatercentenary of the discovery of the Pacific. On February 6th, President Wilson pushed a gold button in Washington, which set the mechanical exhibits in motion. The location extended for about two and a half miles along San Francisco Bay. Eleven splendid buildings housed the exhibits.

THE OCCUPATION OF HAITI

American control of the finances of Santo Domingo, under the Roosevelt arrangement of 1905, was challenged by President Jiménez in 1916, and the naval forces took over the Dominican government. When the republic of Haiti refused to permit establishment of a similar financial protectorate, Marines were landed in December, 1914. Under our military occupancy the Haitian government was stabilized and a new constitution drafted. The occupation met with resistance which was finally stamped out by the Marines and the newly organized Haitian gendarmerie. The picture shows a street in Port-au-Prince.

THE FUTILE CHASE OF VILLA

Huerta's successor as Mexican President, Carranza, was opposed by the bandit chief, Pancho Villa who, during Wilson's period of "Watchful Waiting" on the Mexican situation, met our troops on the border under friendly circumstances, and below is shown with Brigadier General Pershing. But on March 10, 1916, a horde of Villistas raided Columbus, New Mexico, killing soldiers and citizens. Pershing was sent with a punitive expedition to catch the bandits, but the wily Villa eluded pursuit in the mountain fastnesses south of the border. The expedition was withdrawn, and Carranza gained temporary control of Mexico's turbulent politics.

314

PURCHASE OF THE VIRGIN ISLANDS

The process of building up a protective system of naval stations and strategic points to guard the Panama Canal from the east was augmented on January 17, 1917, when the United States purchased the Virgin Island group, guarding the northeastern entrance of the Caribbean. The kingdom of Denmark, which had owned them, was paid $25,000,000, and the inhabitants of the islands, of whom 90 percent are Negroes, were placed under the government of an American naval officer. Above is a street scene in St. Thomas.

THE GALVESTON FLOOD: WRECKAGE

A West Indian hurricane, blowing at the rate of 135 miles an hour, struck the prosperous city of Galveston, Texas, on September 8, 1900, and caused a loss of life estimated at 6,000, and property damage of $15,000,000. Waters of the Gulf of Mexico, whipped to fury by the wind, flooded the streets to a depth higher than a man's head. The nation poured assistance to the stricken survivors and distribution of relief was supervised by troops, hastily sent to the scene of disaster.

316

ASSASSINATION OF McKINLEY

While shaking hands with visitors to the Pan-American Exposition at Buffalo, on September 6, 1901, President McKinley was shot twice and fatally wounded by Leon Czolgosz, a Russian-Polish anarchist; who had carried a pistol under a handkerchief wrapped around his hand. The President died September 14th, Vice-President Theodore Roosevelt thereupon taking the oath as President. Czolgosz was duly tried, found guilty of murder and executed. The photograph, one of McKinley's last, shows him at the Exposition the day before he was shot.

MAN CONQUERS THE AIR

Practical aviation started December 17, 1903, when, in the presence of five spectators, the Wright brothers, Orville and Wilbur, made the first flights in a controllable heavier-than-air machine at Kitty Hawk, North Carolina. At the same time the Wrights were experimenting, Samuel P. Langley was also working on his aërodrome but his machine did not leave the ground till years afterward, and then possibly with some mechanisms not developed by him at the time.

BURNING OF THE "GENERAL SLOCUM"

A terrible disaster which shocked the entire country was the burning of the excursion steamer *General Slocum* on June 15, 1904, in the Hell Gate passage of the East River at New York City. Out of about 1800 passengers, over 1000, mostly women and children out to enjoy a picnic and a day on the water, lost their lives. The boat was old and unseaworthy, and lifeboats and life preservers in wretched condition. The captain was later convicted of criminal negligence. The photograph shows the vessel as she lay on the river's bottom, her superstructure still smouldering.

SAN FRANCISCO EARTHQUAKE AND FIRE

On April 18, 1906, an earthquake never before equaled in violence in the United States struck the city of San Francisco. Soon afterward fires broke out all over the city and for the next three days it was a raging inferno. Troops dynamited large areas in an effort to stop the flames. Said a New York newspaper: "She is the most bunged-up town that ever was. But the spirit of her is enough to bring tears to an American's eyes." Within a year the stricken section was being rebuilt in a new and more beautiful form.

NORTH POLE DISCOVERED

The flag of the United States was planted on top of the world on April 6, 1909, by Commander Robert E. Peary, after years of futile efforts by other explorers to attain the Pole. Worldwide acclaim greeted the exploit, although Dr. Frederick Cook, a Brooklyn scientist, disputed Peary's priority. Ultimately Perry's claim was upheld, Cook's discredited. The photograph shows Peary on the *Roosevelt*, the ship that carried him to the North.

321

HALLEY'S COMET: JOHN DOE STUDIES ASTRONOMY

During April, 1910, the periodic 75 year visibility of Halley's Comet, a heavenly body of extraordinary brilliance, was attended by widespread publicity and consequent popular interest of an unprecedented sort. The comet became the theme of articles, conversation, and even comedy, as well as of unusual scientific activity. Due to technical progress, a wealth of data on the infrequent visitor was obtained by the great observatories, and the man in the street given a glimpse of worlds beyond his own.

SINKING OF THE "TITANIC"

Westward bound on her maiden voyage, the great liner *Titanic*, largest of its day, struck an iceberg in the North Atlantic on April 14, 1912, and sank with a loss of about 1000 persons. America and Europe were plunged into mourning, but thrilled by reports of heroism aboard the sinking ship. Wireless telegraphy was credited with the summoning of aid where in the past the number of those saved might have been negligible. The photographs show survivors being picked up by the *Carpathia*.

THE INCIDENT AT SARAJEVO

The assassination, on June 28, 1914, of the Archduke Franz Ferdinand, heir to the Austrian throne, and his wife while visiting Sarajevo in Bosnia, proved to be the match that started the European conflagration. Holding Serbian revolutionists responsible for the murder, Austria declared war. Russia mobilized, and Germany thereupon declared war on Russia. France, Russia's ally, became embroiled. The German invasion of Belgium brought Great Britain into the conflict. Soon most of Europe was under arms. The illustration shows the Archduke and Duchess a few minutes before they were slain.

SINKING OF THE "LUSITANIA"

NOTICE!

TRAVELLERS intending to embark on the Atlantic voyage are reminded that a state of war exists between Germany and her allies and Great Britain and her allies; that the zone of war includes the waters adjacent to the British Isles; that, in accordance with formal notice given by the Imperial German Government, vessels flying the flag of Great Britain, or of any of her allies, are liable to destruction in those waters and that travellers sailing in the war zone on ships of Great Britain or her allies do so at their own risk.

IMPERIAL GERMAN EMBASSY
WASHINGTON, D. C., APRIL 22, 1915.

When 114 American men, women, and children perished in the torpedoing of the giant Cunarder *Lusitania* off the Old Head of Kinsale, Ireland, on May 7, 1915, the entire nation was aroused. Altogether 1153 aboard the liner perished when she fell prey to a German U-Boat. On the morning she sailed, the above notice appeared in American newspapers. President Wilson sent a note on May 13th, asking the German Government to disavow the sinking. The German reply deprecated the loss of American lives, but denied responsibility. The picture was the last one of the vessel, taken when she was stopped by a British merchant cruiser and given instructions as to how best to evade the submarines.

THE FORD PEACE EXPEDITION

One of the most amazing, in retrospect, efforts to end the war was undertaken by Henry Ford in 1915. Although not an active pacifist he was convinced by others that he could put an end to the great European conflict if the right gesture were made. He chartered the ship *Oscar II* and sailed to Christiania, Norway, whence, finally convinced that the war must run its course, he returned home.

326

PREPAREDNESS, AND A FAMOUS CASE

Some far-sighted persons realized before 1917 that we should prepare for war. Meetings and parades were held to further this cause, during one of which in San Francisco on July 22, 1916, a bomb exploded killing six people. Thomas Mooney, a labor leader, was sentenced to death for the crime. The sentence was never carried out and Mooney is still in jail claiming, among other things, that he watched the parade from the roof shown in this picture.

WARRING ON A NEUTRAL

Due to the tight British blockade, Germany and Austria were unable to obtain supplies from the United States, while the Allies secured them easily. A series of mysterious outrages, such as the Black Tom explosion below. finding of bombs on munition ships consigned to Allied ports, and blowing up of bridges on the Canadian border, led to a Secret Service investigation. A letter from Dr. Dumba, Austrian ambassador at Washington, was intercepted, revealing plots to disorganize the supplying of the Allies. On demand of the State Department, Dumba was recalled, and with him the German attachés, Captains Von Papen and Boy-Ed.

328

WILSON'S REËLECTION AND UNRESTRICTED SUBMARINE WARFARE

Reelected on the slogan of "He kept us out of war," President Wilson was confronted on January 31, 1917, with Germany's declaration of unrestricted submarine warfare against all ships, regardless of nationality, entering the war zone. This breach of a previous pledge not to destroy merchant ships without warning or saving of human lives the President met by breaking off diplomatic relations with Germany. The President then ordered the arming of our merchant ships. The picture shows the President in his second inaugural parade.

READING THE WAR MESSAGE

Night in the House Chamber at the Capitol, April 2, 1917. In ringing tones the President declared that the "irresponsible German government has cast aside all considerations of humanity" and that its recent actions had been "nothing less than war against the government and people of the United States." "The world must be made safe for democracy . . ." The Senate by a vote of 86 to 6, the House by 373 to 50 (after a sixteen-hour debate) passed the resolution declaring war on Germany early in the morning of Good Friday, April 6, 1917.

THE SELECTIVE DRAFT

On recommendation of the General Staff, Congress on May 18, 1917, passed the Selective Service Act, requiring all males between the ages of 21 and 31 to register for selective military service. Of the first numbers drafted, about half were retained and sent to sixteen huge base camps in as many states. The National Guard, mustered into Federal service, occupied sixteen others. Parades of the men chosen in the draft were held in many cities before their departure for the training camps.

BOARD 151

TRAINING CAMPS

The speed with which raw citizens were given the funda-mental war training was amazing. The army command emphasized, among other things, three principles in the training of American soldiers: they should be drilled to fight without interlarding with foreign troops, they should be expert in the use of the bayonet, and the artillery should be expert in marksmanship. In a word, the recruits were trained for offensive, independent fighting.

332

SAYING GOOD-BY

There had been nothing since the Civil War to compare with the wave of patriotic frenzy that swept the country as the troops were bade farewell for the last time. Despite recent attempts to discredit both our motives for entering the conflict and the agencies which stirred these motives, it remains true that we could only have avoided war by ignoring offensive acts against us the like of which few neutrals had ever before been subjected to. Popular enthusiasms at the time, including those of the women, were for the war.

BUILDING A MERCHANT MARINE: HOG ISLAND

From January to July, 1917, the U-boats took fearful toll of the world's shipping. To counteract this loss, the United States Shipping Board organized the Emergency Fleet Corporation and every shipyard in the country was put at top speed. By standardizing designs, inland steel plants turned out parts for these ships, assembly going on at seaboard points such as Hog Island, shown above, with six ships often being launched in a day.

334

THE LIBERTY LOANS

The cost of the war put an unprecedented burden of taxation on the nation, and to meet this, unprecedented taxes were necessary, culminating in the House Revenue Bill of the autumn of 1918 calling for six billion dollars. In May, 1917, the Government offered two billion dollars' worth of its bonds to the general public at $3\frac{1}{2}$ per cent, in the First Liberty Loan. Like the four others that followed, it was oversubscribed. The bonds were sold in units of as little as $50, and there were few people who did not invest their savings in them. The President is shown parading in the cause of the 4th Loan.

THE TRANSATLANTIC FERRY

Protected by the convoy system perfected by the Navy, thousands of American troops were safely transported to France and back again in one of the war's greatest mass movements. Among the huge liners were many ex-German ships, seized after long internment Although their crews had wrecked their engines, American workmen reconditioned them successfully Towering among them was the *Vaterland*, shown here, largest ship of its day, re-named the *Leviathan*.

"LAFAYETTE, WE ARE HERE!"

The military power of the West set foot on French soil in the person of the commander-in-chief of the American Expeditionary Force, General John J. Pershing, when he stepped ashore at Boulogne, in 1917. Shortly afterward he won his first battle when he successfully opposed the proposal of the Allied staff to apportion American troops to various combatant armies, thus preserving the integrity of the American Army as a fighting unit.

UNITED STATES SIGNAL CORPS PHOTO.

THE AMERICANS COME

Of the 2,000,000 United States troops who made the voyage to the war zone in long columns of transports only a few hundreds were lost at sea. This was the great part played by the Navy in the war. The most serious single incident was the loss of the Cunard steamship *Tuscania*, torpedoed off the coast of Ireland in February, 1918, when 175 Americans were drowned. The rest of the men aboard the vessel were rescued by the convoying vessels.

THE LAFAYETTE ESCADRILLE

Many young Americans whose sympathies were with the French before America entered the war, offered their services as aviators in the French Army, forming a unit known as the Lafayette Escadrille, which earned a name for courageous and resourceful fighting against the German airmen. Norman Prince was most active in its organization, and Raoul Lufbery became one of its most famous flyers. With America's entry into the conflict, many transferred to the American air service. In January, 1918, the organization became a part of the American Army.

THE YANKS' FIRST BLOW: CANTIGNY

The doughboy had his first taste of battle at Cantigny. To the First Division went the credit for capture of this heavily fortified position. The military importance of the victory was not great but its moral effect was. It showed that the American soldier had been soundly trained, that he was reliable under fire, and it foreshadowed his work in the Argonne.

CHÂTEAU THIERRY AND BELLEAU WOOD

The last of May and early June, 1918, was one of the most critical periods of the war. The Germans were making their final attempt to break the Allied lines and open a way to Paris. In this engagement the Americans played an important part. First, on May 31st and June 1st, they prevented the Germans from crossing the Marne at Château Thierry; then they checked the advance on the Paris road itself, and ended by taking the strongly defended position in Belleau Wood. The latter was a machine gun and bayonet fight, a type of work in which Americans proved, throughout the war, to excel.

341

SOISSONS TURNS THE TIDE

By the middle of July the French and Americans, the German drive checked, were ready for the ordeal of a counter-offensive. Orders to attack were secretly given. The troops were tense. Now would come the real test of Americans to conduct successfully a crushing offensive. On July 18th it began on the flank between Soissons and Château Thierry. In the five days of terrific fighting that followed the Americans and French suffered great loss, but the Germans were swept out of their trenches and in retreat. Those days were the turning point of the war. The photograph shows German dead in a sunken road far in the rear from which the enemy was driven on the second day.

342

WIPING OUT THE ST. MIHIEL SALIENT

Since 1914, the Germans had managed to hold a vast triangle of French territory jutting twenty miles from the Lorraine border with its apex at St. Mihiel, on the Meuse. Since July, Foch had been on the offensive. He determined to keep on it till the war was over. Sensing that he would strike at St. Mihiel, Von Hindenburg gave orders to evacuate the salient, but his commanders were slow and on September 12th Pershing struck. The photograph shows troops going toward the front.

RESULTS AT ST. MIHIEL

The artillery began pounding the enemy lines at 1 A.M. At 5 A.M. the rolling barrage began, with the Americans going "over the top," to follow it. The enemy barbed wire was cut, and the front trenches reached. Said General Pershing: "At the cost of only 7000 casualties, mostly light, we had taken 16,000 prisoners . . . and es-

tablished our lines in a position to threaten Metz. The Allies found (in this first offensive of the American First Army) that they had a formidable army to aid them, and the enemy learned finally that he had one to reckon with." The photograph shows German troops retreating.

344

THE MEUSE-ARGONNE: FIRST PHASE

The supreme effort of the Americans was the Meuse-Argonne offensive between late September and the Armistice. On its success hinged Foch's plans, now that he had straightened out his lines and was ready to deliver the final blow. In the last days of September and early October, green American troops went forward ten miles, penetrating the German second line of defense, although with terrific loss. It was the first phase of the battle.

THE MEUSE-ARGONNE: SECOND PHASE

The second phase included the struggle for the Argonne forest and saw the most terrific fighting that an American army had been called on to face in all its history. The Germans were resolved that wherever else they gave way, this great sector of the line, which had been theirs since 1914, would be held. Dying for every foot of ground conquered, the Americans went forward, plunging into the Argonne forest. It was there that the Lost Battalion advanced too far and was cut off from retreat. The attack reached its high point with the capture of Blanc Mont, in which the fury of the Americans was outstanding.

346

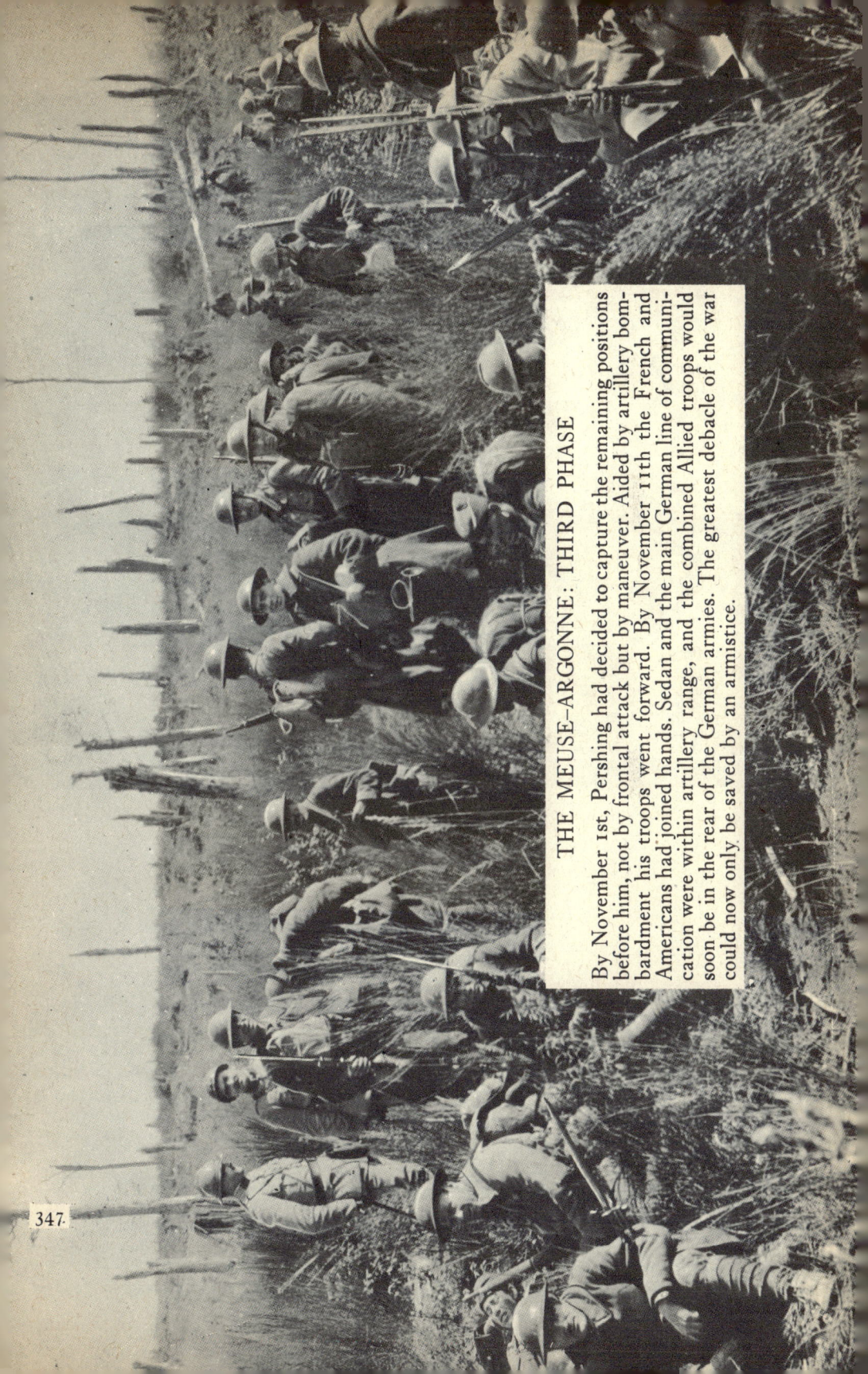

THE MEUSE-ARGONNE: THIRD PHASE

By November 1st, Pershing had decided to capture the remaining positions before him, not by frontal attack but by maneuver. Aided by artillery bombardment his troops went forward. By November 11th the French and Americans had joined hands. Sedan and the main German line of communication were within artillery range, and the combined Allied troops would soon be in the rear of the German armies. The greatest debacle of the war could now only be saved by an armistice.

THE ARMISTICE

The German high command now was forced to admit what they had long secretly known. The end was at hand. Armistice was declared on the 11th, amid scenes in the trenches that ranged from blank wonder and dazed inability to realize that bloodshed was at last over to scenes of wild celebration. To every soldier the ending of the war meant a turning-point in his life. Said Pershing of the Meuse-Argonne battle: "... You battered against the pivot of the enemy line ... a position fortified by four years of labor designed to render it impregnable. ... The achievement of the First Army ... is scarcely to be equaled in American history. ..."

THE NAVY'S PART

Preceded by a destroyer fleet which arrived May 4th at Queenstown, Ireland, the battleship divisions of the United States Navy were sent across the Atlantic to coöperate with the British Grand Fleet at its North Sea bases. Although our battleships fought no engagement with the German fleet, their presence aided in nullifying German sea power for the remainder of the war. Thousands of sailors aboard them witnessed the final surrender of the German warships and submarines, treacherously scuttled by their crews afterward at Scapa Flow. The picture shows Admiral Beatty and British tars welcoming the ships of the United States at Scapa Flow.

COURTESY UNITED STATES NAVY DEPARTMENT.

ARMISTICE DAY AT HOME

News of the signing of the Armistice brought an outpouring of the people into the streets of all American cities rejoicing at the end of the war. Men in uniform were hailed with enthusiasm, total strangers exchanged delighted handshakes. The Kaiser was "licked," Yankee-fashion, and the formidable German army had been taught to respect an aroused United States. Before homes where a gold star in the window signified one had fallen for his country, reverent groups gathered. The picture below shows Fifth Avenue in New York on November 11, 1918.

THE BIG FOUR

Knowing that his proposed Covenant of the League of Nations, one of his Fourteen Points, was being discountenanced by a hostile Congress behind him, President Wilson sailed for the Peace Conference on December 4, 1918, and on arrival at Paris commenced work on the Treaty with (left to right) Orlando of Italy, Lloyd George of Great Britain, and Clemenceau of France. The enthusiasm with which he was hailed throughout Europe has never been accorded any other individual American. He succeeded in having a committee appointed to draw up his Covenant as an integral part of the treaty of peace, more than a dozen nations expressing immediate approval, then returned to face the Congressional opposition.

HOOVER, AND RELIEF OF THE STARVING

The plight of helpless women and children in invaded Belgium resulted in the formation of the Belgian Relief Commission, which under the able direction of Herbert Hoover saved thousands of lives by its efficient distribution of food supplies. Later American relief was extended to post-war Germany and Russia. During the conflict, Serbia and other nations were helped by American generosity. With the entrance of this country into the war, Hoover was appointed Food Administrator to conserve national resources in foodstuffs. He inaugurated wheatless, meatless, and sugarless days, and directed the sending of $2,000,000,000 worth of food to Europe during 1918. He is shown here, accompanied by John D. Rockefeller, Jr., in one of the war-time cafeterias.

352

"SEE AMERICA THIRST"

This parody of an advertising catch-phrase became popular with the advent of national prohibition. Its regrettable effects on our national life would probably have been avoided had not war hysteria made it possible for the extreme temperance advocates to popularize their program. Transportation of intoxicants was also forbidden, and citizens were even searched for hip-flasks, as shown above. Prohibition was embodied in the Constitution as the Eighteenth Amendment. The era of the prohibition agent, the bootlegger, and the speakeasy was ushered into the national life.

THE PEACE CONFERENCE

On June 28, 1919, in the same Hall of Mirrors at Versailles where King William of Prussia humbled a prostrate France in 1871, the representatives of Germany signed the Treaty of Peace of the Great War, by which Alsace-Lorraine was restored to France, and other territories to Belgium, Denmark, and Poland. Germany agreed to surrender most of her fleet, to demolish her fortifications, abolish her air force, and reduce her army to a police force of 100,000 men. An initial payment of 20 billion marks to pay for damage in regions occupied by her troops was exacted, and she was compelled, under protest, to assume responsibility for the war. The new German Republic was stunned by the terms.

WILSON STUMPS FOR THE LEAGUE

The Covenant of the League of Nations, embodied in the Peace Treaty, was the stumbling-block of President Wilson's plans when Congress acted. The Treaty was rejected, the Republicans in Congress calling for amendments to the Covenant, which they deemed dangerous to national sovereignty, and the Democrats holding out for no changes. Convinced that he could not obtain ratification, the President appealed to the nation in a speech-making tour of the principal cities. On September 26, 1919, he was stricken with paralysis which made him an invalid for the remaining four and one-half years of his life. The picture was the first "close-up," which the President allowed to be taken of him after his illness, and although it removed the doubts of some as to the seriousness of his affliction, it certainly did not show him a well man.

THE BOSTON POLICE STRIKE

In September, 1919, the police force of Boston, after negotiating unsuccessfully for a pay increase, went on strike, thinking to bring the city to terms when it found itself without police protection. The strike was broken through the intervention of Governor Calvin Coolidge, who placed Massachusetts National Guardsmen in charge after rioting had occurred. The successful breaking of the strike, credited to Coolidge, brought him national fame, and was a potent factor in bringing about his nomination for Vice-President in 1920.

WOMEN GET THE VOTE

In sharp contrast to the methods of their English cousins, American women had been peacefully agitating for the right to vote since the days of Susan B. Anthony. In the twentieth century the movement spread, characterized by parades, picketings of the White House, and heckling of public men opposing the trend. By 1916 a dozen states had extended the franchise and both Presidential candidates declared themselves in favor. In 1919 Congress passed the Nineteenth Amendment which was proclaimed August 26, 1920, in time to allow women to vote in the Presidential election of that year.

357

THE POST–WAR DEPRESSION: 5,000,000 UNEMPLOYED

Soon after the war boom in industry a reaction set in, culminating in the depression of 1921. Wartime wages could not be maintained, and this tendency labor resisted strongly. Nation-wide strikes followed, especially in the railroad and coal industries. By 1921 there were more than 5,000,000 unemployed. However, by 1923 the country had begun the upswing which was to continue, almost uninterrupted, till 1929. The picture was taken in New York in 1922.

IMMIGRATION RESTRICTION: THE LAND OF PROMISE

The laws of 1921 and 1924 gave the United States a cohesive immigration policy at long last. Organized labor had long advocated restriction, but capital had opposed it, fearing it would bring high wages. The drastic reduction of 1921 was aimed at preventing exploitation of the country by unnaturalized aliens, and to hold back what threatened to be a flood of immigrants from the war-torn nations of Europe. But this law did not go far enough and in 1924 was passed the epoch-making act which fixed the annual quota of each nation at 2% of its immigrants to the United States in 1890. To all intents, the flood was shut off. The law superseded the "Gentlemen's Agreement" and infuriated Japan by excluding Asiatics. The photograph shows immigrants on Ellis Island in New York Harbor gazing toward "the land of promise."

NAVAL DISARMAMENT CONFERENCE

Summoned by President Harding, delegates from eight European and Asiatic powers met at Washington on November 11, 1921, to discuss naval disarmament. A holiday of ten years for new construction was agreed upon, and the tonnage of the three leading nations was set at a 5:5:3 ratio for Great Britain, the United States, and Japan. Hailed as a step toward peace, the Conference was in reality a manifestation of the isolationism of the Twenties and, repudiated by Japan a decade later, it dangerously weakened our Navy in the face of the growing military mights of Germany and Japan.

THE DAWES REPARATIONS COMMISSION

One of the controversial post-war problems was the matter of the war debts. At first, the British war debt to the United States was settled by an agreement spreading repayment of the amount owed over a long-term period. France, Italy, and Belgium, however, made their repayments contingent on Germany's paying indemnity to them. The constantly reiterated plaint of Germany that she could not pay led to the appointment by the Allied Reparation Commission of General Charles G. Dawes, Owen D. Young, and H. M. Robinson, below, to study the Reich's condition. The "Dawes Plan," was evolved whereby long-term payments of sums from earnings of German railroads and industries were coupled with a loan from the United States to assist the defeated country, and supervision of payments was placed in the hands of an American. Thus did the United States lend money to bankrupt Germany in the hope that she would pay the European allies, and that they would in turn pay America. The hope was realized to only a limited extent, for eventually another scheme, the Young Plan, had to be evolved, and finally came general European repudiation.

THE McNARY–HAUGEN BILLS

As a class the American farmer profited enormously during the war, by reason of the fact that the world was his market and the price he received for his products rose to unprecedented levels. With the early 1920's came the inevitable bursting of the bubble. Loth to accept virtually half of what he had become accustomed to, a "Farm Bloc" appeared in Congress which sought on his behalf to solve the question by national legislation. The McNary-Haugen bill providing for creation of a National Agricultural Export Commission with large capital resources to buy up farm surpluses and sell them abroad was passed in February, 1927, after three years' deliberation, but was vetoed by President Coolidge. A second bill in the next Congress to put the government into the farm business was also vetoed. Below, Senator Charles L. McNary, of Oregon, and Congressman Gilbert N. Haugen.

THE TEAPOT DOME SCANDALS

An outgrowth of the Harding administration was the scandal centering around Albert B. Fall, ex-Secretary of the Interior, which came as a result of his leasing naval oil reserve lands at Teapot Dome, Wyoming, and Elk Hills, California, to the Sinclair and Doheny interests. Fall had accepted a loan of $100,000 from Doheny without interest or security. Convicted of accepting a bribe, Fall was sentenced to a year's imprisonment. The Senate committee, of which Smoot and Lenroot were members, is shown above investigating the case which, in its ramifications, including that of jury-shadowing, dragged its sordid story through the courts for several years.

LOS ANGELES IS PREPARED to WELCOME
AMERICAN LEGION in 1931

DETROIT 1931

THE SOLDIERS' BONUS

Discontent among ex-service men grew as the returned doughboys compared their war pay with that earned by factory and shipyard workers during the war. In 1924 an "Adjusted Compensation Bill" was passed in the form of paid-up twenty-year insurance policies maturing in 1945 and averaging $1590 per veteran. Vetoed by President Coolidge, the measure was passed over his veto on May 19, 1924. Following, the bonus had been a political battleground, especially during depres-

sion years. President Hoover addressed the American Legion National Convention in 1930 (above) and again in 1931. At the latter, the demand for immediate payment of the bonus reached such proportions that he explained to the delegates that "the path of service to the nation" lay in not placing any additional financial burden on this country. However, Congress on January 27, 1936, passed a bill for immediate payment over the veto of the President.

364

THE MARINES IN NICARAGUA ONCE MORE

Hardly had the Marines left Nicaragua in 1925 than that turbulent country was again in the throes of a revolution. The president and vice-president were exiled, but returned in 1926 to fight the régime of Adolfo Diaz, the Conservative incumbent. The United States furnished arms and munitions to the Diaz regime. In April, 1927, when the ex-president's army neared the capital, the United States compelled both factions to terminate hostilities. A guerilla warfare followed between the Marines and Sandino, an isolated rebel leader, whose forces were ultimately routed, but who remained uncaptured.

THE COMING OF RADIO

The daily habits of the nation were destined to be changed when the first commercial radio broadcast went on the air from Station KDKA, by employees of the Westinghouse Company at East Pittsburgh, in 1920. Music was furnished by phonograph records. The broadcast of the Dempsey-Carpentier fight in 1921 received only limited attention, but from 1921 to 1922 the new means of entertainment and news dissemination captured public attention and the country went radio-mad. Another industry, recreation, and educational influence had come into being. The picture shows an early experimental broadcasting station in the garage of Dr. Conrad's home in Pittsburgh.

THE GANGSTER ERA: CAPONE

Disrespect for the prohibition law reached a climax during the prosperous years. Outstanding among gangsters was "Scarface" Al Capone, whose illicit activities terrorized Chicago, and whose wealth enabled him to maintain the Florida mansion shown above. His skill in eluding direct responsibility, and at the same time enjoying his wealth, was illustrated when the Miami police tagged him for their Rogues' Gallery, yet could not jail him. Eventually he was convicted, not for the crimes which had terrorized Chicago, but for income-tax evasion—a federal offense.

THE NATION PROSPERS

From 1925 to 1929 the general prosperity of the country passed all records. Treasury surpluses were shown, despite slashing reductions in federal taxes and large payments on the national debt. Typical of the nation-wide enthusiasm was Chicago, which spread many millions of dollars over new tracts of land. In every American city new buildings rose, municipal improvements were made, and plans laid for a future that never arrived.

SIGNING THE KELLOGG–BRIAND PACT

On the tenth anniversary of the United States entry into the World War, the French Minister of Foreign Affairs, Aristide Briand, proposed both governments should sign a pact outlawing war and agreeing to settle all disputes pacifically. The pact was signed by Secretary of State Kellogg and President Coolidge January 17, 1928. Later Secretary Kellogg obtained the signatures of sixty-two nations to a similar proposal. The pact was to be flouted later by Japan's invasion of Manchuria.

COOLIDGE REFUSES TO RUN

In August, 1927, Calvin Coolidge, while on vacation in the West, announced, "I do not choose to run for President in 1928." The nation misjudged the strength of the determination that was behind this homely New England phraseology. Coolidge's administration was marked by continuing business prosperity and by his personal popularity, in great measure due to his refusal to embrace any idea not readily understood by the average man. The picture is typical of the many homely poses in which the President allowed himself to be photographed.

RACE RIOTS IN CHICAGO

In July, 1919, resentment at the moving of high-waged Negro workers into white residential districts in Chicago flared into a race riot. Both blacks and whites were killed. The rioting ended only after police and troops had removed the threatened families to safety. Above, white children cheering as a Negro's home is fired, and police removing one of the offenders to safety. Uprisings against Negro expansion also took place in other cities during this period.

WALL STREET EXPLOSION

At noon on a warm day in September, 1920, a drooping old horse drew a wagon into Wall Street and stopped before the United States Assay Office, across the street from J. P. Morgan & Company. An instant later there was a terrific explosion. Wall Street, from Nassau to William, was a shambles. Thirty-five were killed and more than a hundred injured. Direct responsibility for the tragedy, attributed to anti-capitalistic agitators, has never been definitely established.

KU KLUX KLAN: THE FIERY CROSS ABROAD AGAIN

Taking advantage of post-war emotionalism in the early 1920's, a group of Georgians revived the old Ku Klux Klan of the Civil War reconstruction period, and by modern publicity methods gained thousands of followers who were made to contribute heavily for the privilege of wearing the ghostly raiment of the Invisible Empire. Tarrings, featherings, floggings, and finally murders were attributed to the Klan's anti-Negro-Catholic-Jewish creed, and popular resentment and riots at Klan meetings followed. The movement spread throughout the eastern United States. Dissension broke out among its officials and the movement dwindled to isolated groups in remote districts.

THE ADVENT OF COOLIDGE

The illustration shows Calvin Coolidge entering the temporary executive quarters in the Senate Office Building as President, two days after Harding's death. While returning from a trip to Alaska, Harding had died at San Francisco on August 2, 1923. When Coolidge heard of his death he was visiting his boyhood home in Vermont. There, his father, a justice of the peace, by the light of an oil lamp in the parlor, swore his son in as Chief Executive. The dramatic quality of that scene in the New England farmhouse appealed to the traditional American feeling for things homely.

DESTRUCTION OF THE "SHENANDOAH"

Activities of the German Zeppelins in sea patrol service during the war prompted the Navy Department to undertake experiments in rigid airships. The *Los Angeles*, a non-combatant ship, was purchased from the Zeppelin Works, and made the transatlantic flight to the great naval hangar at Lakehurst, New Jersey. The first American rigid airship, the *Shenandoah*, was built at Akron, Ohio. After many successful flights, the craft was totally wrecked in an equinoctial storm over Ava, Ohio, September 3, 1925, its commander and thirteen others being killed.

THE EUCHARISTIC CONGRESS IN CHICAGO

One of the most remarkable gatherings in the United States for a religious event took place during the Eucharistic Congress at Chicago, June, 1926, when Catholics from all over the country, to a number estimated at the time at 170,000, flocked to that city for a week of solemn observance. The Congress was accorded the honor of a Papal Legate, Cardinal Bonzano. Above is a view of Soldiers' Field with the high altar at the left where the Cardinal celebrated mass before the devout throng.

FIRST FLORIDA HURRICANE

Spurred by the example of Southern California, the state of Florida attracted thousands in a real estate boom in the early 1920's. The climate, accessibility by automobile, and public willingness to take a chance on liberal credit, led to gigantic developments. Miami quintupled her population between 1920 and 1925. On September 17–18, 1926, a West Indian hurricane struck Miami and the adjacent coast, wrecked the ornate Venetian residences, hurled ships and yachts into the streets, left a trail of 370 killed, and caused a property damage of $100,000,000. The Florida boom, one of the signs of the times, collapsed. Hardly over this first disaster, Florida experienced another hurricane on almost the same date in 1928. Many times more persons were killed by it, but the property damage was much less.

THE SACCO-VANZETTI CASE

Fear that Bolshevist doctrines might spread from Russia to the United States, coupled with increased activities of Communists and other radical groups, threw the country into a "Red" scare in the post-war period. All such movements need a "goat," and one came readily to hand in Sacco and Vanzetti, two Italian anarchists. They were sentenced to death for the murder of a South Braintree, Massachusetts, paymaster. The case got world attention. The radical and liberal press at home and abroad was loud in its denunciation of American justice. Governor Fuller and a board of review, however, were adamant, and the two men were electrocuted on August 23, 1927.

THE PRIZE RING LOSES ITS STIGMA

Frowned on in the Nineteenth Century, pugilism became a national fetish after the war. The great throngs, representing all walks of life, that came to see the fights were indicative of a country bursting with paper profits and looking for ways to exhibit its prosperity. The crowds jammed sporting events of every sort all over the country. Even tennis came into "the big money." Subsequently the period was aptly dubbed, "the era of wonderful nonsense." An outstanding event was the return fight between Gene Tunney, champion, and Jack Dempsey, former champion, at Chicago, on September 22, 1927. The illustration shows the famous "long count" when Tunney, floored, had more than ten seconds in which to rise, due to Dempsey's slowness in going to his corner.

379

SINKING OF THE "VESTRIS"

On November 12, 1928, the British steamship *Vestris*, bound from New York to Barbadoes, Rio de Janeiro, and Buenos Aires, ran into a heavy storm off the Virginia Capes and sustained such damage that it sank, carrying down one hundred and ten passengers and crew. In the investigation that followed charges were made that the ship had been allowed to sail from New York with its cargo improperly loaded, causing a heavy list. Others attributed it to damage caused by a hurricane. The picture is one of the most remarkable views of a marine disaster ever photographed.

REPRINTED BY COURTESY OF THE NEW YORK "NEWS."

380

INAUGURATION OF THE AIR MAIL SERVICE

The United States showed the same slowness in carrying the mail by air, despite years of such transportation abroad, that it had in recognizing the epoch-making invention of the Wright brothers. It was not until May 15, 1918, that the first air mail service was begun, a comparatively short "hop," between New York and Washington. Below is shown President Wilson greeting the pioneer pilot at Potomac Field. The flight ushered in the development of the modern air service.

FLIGHT OF THE "NC–4" ACROSS THE ATLANTIC

With a string of warships stationed at intervals along their route in case of trouble, the Navy flying-boats NC–1, NC–3, and NC–4 left Rockaway Beach, New York, May 8, 1919, in an attempt to cross the Atlantic by airplane. They reached Trepassey Bay, Newfoundland, and on May 16th headed for the Azores. Of the three, only the NC–4 made the journey by air, the time being a little more than 15 hours. The NC–1 was forced down and sank, a steamer rescuing the crew. The NC–3 also suffered a mishap, but navigated on the surface to Ponta Delgada safely. The NC–4 afterward flew to Spain and England. Crossing the ocean in heavier-than-air machines had been proved feasible. The photograph shows the start of the three planes from Rockaway Beach.

END OF THE FIRST NON-STOP ATLANTIC FLIGHT

Early transatlantic flights by American aviators often obscure the fact that to Britain belongs the credit for the first non-stop transatlantic airplane journey. On June 14–15, 1919, eight years before Lindbergh's achievement, John Alcock and Arthur W. Brown flew their Vickers-Vimy biplane, similar to a wartime bomber, from St. Johns, Newfoundland, to Clifden, Ireland, in safety. The plane sustained damage in landing, as the pilot brought it down in an Irish bog, but 1960 miles had been flown in a little more than 16 hours.

AROUND THE WORLD BY AIR

Though the Navy made the first transatlantic airplane flight, the Army did its part in a round-the-world flight that made history. Four Douglas biplanes started from Santa Monica, California, March 17, 1924, and headed for Seattle, the official starting point. One plane was forced down in Alaska. The remaining three continued on the trip but one of them was wrecked in attempting to reach Iceland, after Asia and Europe had been successfully spanned. Lieutenants Smith and Nelson piloted the remaining two to Seattle, where they landed on September 28th. The photograph shows the welcoming crowd at Mitchel Field, Long Island, N. Y., one of the stops made near the end of the flight.

384

BYRD FLIES OVER THE NORTH POLE

Another flying achievement was credited to America when Commander Richard E. Byrd and Floyd Bennett, U. S. Navy, took off from King's Bay, near Spitzbergen, on May 9, 1926, and reached the North Pole. They circled it successfully and returned, having covered 1500 miles over the Arctic wastes. Their trip was of geographic value for it showed no new land in the area over which they traveled. The picture shows the Byrd plane returning to Spitzbergen from the flight over the Pole.

LINDBERGH'S FLIGHT TO PARIS

The aviation event which most captured popular fancy in the pioneer years of transatlantic flight was the solo trip of Charles A. Lindbergh from New York to Paris in his Ryan monoplane *Spirit of St. Louis*. He hopped off while more pretentious expeditions were in course of preparation, in the early hours of May 20, 1927. Al-though he encountered bad weather, he landed his craft at Paris, 3610 miles away, in 33 hours and 29 minutes. Above, the landing at Le Bourget airdrome near Paris, with soldiers and gendarmes holding back a wildly enthusiastic crowd.

LINDBERGH REACHES HOME

A Twentieth Century version of a Roman triumph was accorded the modest hero when he arrived in New York from Washington, June 13, 1927. Not the least of the honors accorded him was the fact that a United States warship, the *Memphis,* was sent to bring this private citizen home. The city's greeting was extended by the then popular Mayor, James J. Walker. Soon after Lindbergh, Clarence Chamberlain flew to Germany and Commander Richard E. Byrd to France. These three flights dramatized the modern era of flight. In 1926 Byrd had flown over the North Pole and in 1929 he flew to the South Pole.

THE PANIC OF OCTOBER, 1929

The Belshazzar's Feast of American prosperity was not without some handwriting on the wall. Certain conservative economists had warned against such an orgy of optimism, but it was not until October, 1929, that their warnings were heeded. The Stock Market collapsed, and a stampede to sell stocks set in, 12,800,000 shares being sold October 24th, and 16,400,000 shares October 29th. Fortunes vanished, paper profits were wiped out, and gilt-edged securities sank to record lows. The picture shows the crowd in front of the Stock Exchange during the panic. In the wake of the crash came unemployment, idle factories, bank failures, foreclosures, and falling off in prices generally.

388

BANK FAILURES

One of the first effects on the nation's financial structure, as the depression deepened, was a wave of bank closings, the like of which had never been experienced. It showed the inherent weakness of many of the state banking laws. A notable failure was that of The Bank of the United States, in New York, in December, 1930. It seems probable that the name of the bank induced many ignorant people to deposit their money therein. A crowd is shown in front of one of the institution's many branches.

THE HOOVER MORATORIUM

Not only the United States but virtually the entire world had been sliding down the depression incline for almost two years when President Hoover, in an effort to relieve one of the international difficulties, proposed in June, 1931, a one-year moratorium on payments of all inter-governmental war debts and conditional reparations. The proposal was approved with modifications by France, and later by other interested nations. Undoubtedly the moratorium eased the situation somewhat, but it did not cure the cycle of bad business which had yet to run its complete course. The picture shows Secretary of the Treasury Mellon and Ambassador Edge leaving the Quai d'Orsay in Paris after France had signed the moratorium.

THE RECONSTRUCTION FINANCE CORPORATION

President Hoover sought to halt the depression by asking business not to interrupt its expansion program or reduce wages, by appointing a Cabinet committee to investigate means of reducing unemployment, and by planning for public works, farm relief, and emergency construction. In early 1932, he created the Reconstruction Finance Corporation, with a capital of $2,000,000,000, to make loans to railroads, insurance companies, agricultural associations, banks, and other enterprises. The directors of the corporation, including Charles G. Dawes, who had just resigned as ambassador to Great Britain, are shown above.

THE BONUS ARMY

Several thousand unemployed veterans, at the height of the depression in the spring of 1932, converged on Washington and camped on Government property, demanding immediate payment of the soldier's bonus, not due until 1945. The Washington police, after temporizing, ordered them to move out of the city, and when they refused attempted to evict them. The veterans beat the police off, and troops were called out who routed the malcontents with tear gas and tanks. President Hoover was charged with using American soldiers against impoverished patriots, and the accusation lost him many votes in the November election in which he was defeated for re-election.

© NEWS SYNDICATE CO., INC., FROM ACME.

END OF AN ERA: MAYOR WALKER

Throughout the depression there became manifest a desire to be rid of established political orders, whether Democratic or Republican. This was especially in evidence in cities where municipal finance was beginning to be called to account for maladministration and graft. In New York in 1932 the once popular Mayor and play-boy, James J. Walker, proved vulnerable to attack. Eventually he resigned under fire and left the country.

INSULL: A FIGURE OF THE TIMES

Prior to 1929, despite the anti-trust laws, vast holding corporations grew throughout the country, embracing many major industries. Sale of their shares was widespread, due to popular faith in their future, and certain economic benefits derived from standardization and elimination of waste methods among their subsidiaries. With the stock-market crash, the popular dream vanished and a wave of resentment swept over the country against those who promoted the ambitious schemes. Typical was the case of Samuel Insull, Mid-West utilities magnate, who fled to Europe to escape prosecution, was extradited after a long pursuit, and subsequently acquitted. The picture shows Insull at the Chicago Century of Progress Exposition.

END OF THE NICARAGUAN ADVENTURE

With growing agitation in Congress for their removal and a certain amount of equilibrium attained in the Nicaraguan government, the Marines evacuated that country in January, 1933. Sandino, the rebel leader, whom the sea-soldiers had failed to catch, though they killed many of his followers, at once made peace with President Sacasa but was later kidnaped and murdered. Thus was ended another attempt by the United States to protect its South American interests by force. The picture shows the arrival of the Marines at Quantico in January.

ROOSEVELT INAUGURATED

Herbert Hoover went down to defeat in November, 1932, before an electorate which charged the Republican party for much of the depression and him personally for failure to cure it. The New Deal arrived March 4, 1933, when Franklin Delano Roosevelt was inaugurated. As with Lincoln, his term began during a national crisis with the added burden that 12,000,000 were unemployed throughout the land. The country was in have since claimed might have been averted had the incoming President not refused to coöperate in efforts to stem it. With every bank in the country closed, general panic was averted by Roosevelt's use of the radio to carry into American homes his assurance that the banks would reopen shortly, and a new phase of national life would be entered that would lead out of the economic quagmire.

"BRAIN TRUST"

Shortly after his inauguration, President Roosevelt surrounded himself with a group of confidential advisers, most of them not cabinet members. Some of this group were college professors and the public quickly named the advisers the "Brain Trust." Big business severely criticized the President's action in listening to the theories of men whom industrial leaders believed to be theorists and visionaries. The personnel of the "Brain Trust" underwent changes as the Administration progressed, but the group itself was maintained in the face of much adverse comment. The picture shows Roosevelt, as President-Elect, conferring with Raymond Moley, chief "brain truster," and, until shortly before, of the faculty of Columbia University, at Hyde Park, New York.

GOLD STANDARD ABANDONED

On April 19, 1933, President Roosevelt ordered an embargo on all gold exports, thus officially taking the country off the international gold standard. Earlier in the month he had prohibited the hoarding of gold, while at the time of his temporary closing of the banks he had prohibited the withdrawal of gold or silver for domestic or export trade. Congress validated the President's actions, and invested him with monetary powers to use at his discretion. Above, under heavy guard and at night, gold valued at $750,000,000 being removed from the San Francisco Mint for shipment to Denver.

THE F. E. R. A.: 14,000,000 UNEMPLOYED

The number of men out of work throughout the country reached an all-time high in March, 1933, with about 14,000,000 jobless. An effort was made through the Federal Emergency Relief Administration, in cooperation with the states, to relieve the hardships of these stricken people and their families. Many unemployed, thousands of whom were homeless, established "shanty-towns," on vacant lots in cities, building shacks from cast-off material. The situation was without precedent in the nation's history.

BEER RETURNS

One of the first results of the administration of Franklin D. Roosevelt was the legalization of 3.2 per cent beer. The cry, in part, was that this would raise large revenues and put men to work, but the fact was that the nation wanted an end of prohibition. The appearance of trucks hauling the now-legalized beverages never failed to create interest. Some few horse-drawn trucks went into service just as in "the good old days," but they were mostly for purposes of atmosphere. Many states, foreseeing the end of prohibition, took steps at this early stage to prevent the return of the old-time saloon.

THE CENTURY OF PROGRESS

In the face of the most stringent period, the city of Chicago sounded a note of national optimism with its "Century of Progress" exposition, held in 1933. The great Fair, constructed on artificially made land on the shores of Lake Michigan, glorified the achievements of the Machine Age with buildings expressing the new note in architecture. In contrast to other attempts, immediately previous, to hold "world's fairs," the Chicago venture was a financial success and was repeated the following summer.

COMING OF THE N. R. A.

One of Roosevelt's efforts to end the depression was the National Industrial Recovery Act, which he sponsored, authorizing the President to establish agencies to assist in bringing about recovery. One of these was the National Recovery Administration, which set about placing industry under codes, fixing maximum work weeks, minimum rates of pay, eliminating destructive price competition, and aiming toward establishment of fair business methods. Firms complying with the codes were given the right to display a "Blue Eagle" insignia. The movement was ushered in by parades in many cities, such as the New York one above, showing support of the plan. The fiery General Hugh Johnson as head of the N. R. A. Board soon began taking to himself much of the limelight in Washington.

THE FARM STRIKE

In the Northwest and Middle West the farm situation in 1933 was as bad as that of unemployment in the industrial areas. Unable to obtain even production cost prices for their commodities, farmers in several states staged a form of strike, picketed roads into cities and destroyed truckloads of milk and produce attempting to reach the markets. The movement was broken up by state troops and increased Governmental attention to farm relief.

SOVIET RUSSIA RECOGNIZED

Correspondence between Washington and the U.S.S.R. was made public
before the end of President Roosevelt's first year in office, showing that the
way was being paved for formal recognition of the existing Russian government. On November 16, 1933, recognition took place, the Soviet government binding itself to refrain from interfering in this country's internal
affairs and guaranteeing American rights and religious freedom in Russia.
Above is shown United States Ambassador William C. Bullitt arriving in
Moscow.

THE C.C.C.: CARING FOR JOBLESS YOUTH

To alleviate the plight of thousands of young men out of work, or unable to obtain jobs on leaving school, the Civilian Conservation Corps was created by act of Congress, providing for enlistments at nominal pay for engaging in work of reforestation, flood control, soil erosion protection, and other activities. Money was set aside to finance the conservation work, and by the spring of 1933 thousands of these young men were engaged in the healthful work. The idea of the camps is said to have been President Roosevelt's. In any case it was one of the early triumphs of the "New Deal." The photograph shows the President visiting one of the camps.

REPEAL OF PROHIBITION

"The noble experiment" approached its end when the Lame Duck session of Congress, February 16 and 20, 1933, passed the Twenty-first Amendment to the Constitution, repealing the Eighteenth. The nation responded quickly to the opportunity to express its opinion on a law that could not have been and never was enforced. By December, Prohibition was in the past. When the Utah state Senate ratified repeal and thereby wrote "Finis" to an era which had resulted in widespread disrespect for law and the development of a new criminal class, legal liquor again began to flow across the nation's bars amid scenes of genuine and, on the whole, restrained celebration.

THE NEW DEAL REACHES CONGRESS

At the opening of Congress in January, 1934, President Roosevelt placed before it his program for the "New Deal." It called for reorganization of the political and economic system so that the Government would thereafter take an active part in coöperating with business to bring about national stability. The President's outline covered three phases—relief, "reflation," and reform.

THE A. A. A. AND THE FARMER

The Agricultural Adjustment Administration was another of the major measures instituted by the New Deal. It concentrated on restriction of acreage and production of agricultural commodities in order to provide increased agricultural purchasing power, orderly liquidation of joint-stock land banks, and other results beneficial to the farmer. It was instituted in May, 1933. At that time farm mortgages were being foreclosed; and commodity prices were about 50 per cent of those before the war.

THE P. W. A.: A HOUSING PROJECT

The Public Works Administration was another channel through which the administration struck at the depression. It was allotted $3,300,000,000, partly in grants, partly in loans, to be spent on public works, either Federal or of community benefit, and gave employment to thousands otherwise idle. A typical example of its accomplishments is shown above in the gigantic housing project completed in the Bronx section of New York City, to accommodate families at low rents in comfortable, healthful apartments.

DROUGHT IN THE WEST

Early in the spring of 1934 a drought appeared in the Northwest and spread rapidly to the Southeast, South, and Southwest. By the end of May it had developed into the worst on record. The feed and forage shortage resulted in the deaths of many thousands of livestock, and wrought untold misery on the farmers, until the arrival of benefit payments in the crop adjustment program and the wholesale purchase of drought-cattle stocks by the AAA somewhat alleviated the situation.

THE SAN FRANCISCO GENERAL STRIKE

One phenomenon that set off the depression years from similar previous periods was the absence of a series of widespread and prolonged strikes, with inevitable violence, bloodshed, and death, following in their wake. This does not mean that such strikes as there were, were not serious. The most widespread was the general strike in San Francisco in the summer of 1934. The photograph shows a protest mass meeting in the Civil Center during the height of the strike.

THE N. R. A. DECISION

While the Administration was contending for extension of the N. R. A. the Supreme Court on May 27, 1935, rendered a unanimous decision declaring the act to be unconstitutional, asserting that it unlawfully delegated to others authority vested in Congress and that as applied to intrastate operation it usurped power belonging to the states. The decision upset a primary essential of the New Deal program, nullifying all industrial codes then in effect. Donald Richberg, Chairman of the Industrial Recovery Board, is shown on May 20th before the House Ways and Means Committee, pleading for the long-term continuance of the N. R. A. Act.

GEORGE WASHINGTON BRIDGE

One of the outstanding engineering feats of the world was the building of the George Washington suspension bridge over the Hudson River above New York City. The channel span, measuring 3500 feet, will remain the longest in the world until the new one across the Golden Gate at San Francisco is completed. It was a far cry from this monster with its speeding automobiles to the crowds rioting on the Brooklyn Bridge for fear it would fall. The photograph shows the bridge on opening day in October, 1931.

LINDBERGH KIDNAPING

While on a "goodwill" flight to Mexico, Lindbergh met, and some time after married, the daughter of Ambassador Dwight W. Morrow. On the night of March 1, 1932, the entire world was horrified by the kidnaping of their baby son from their home (white spot at extreme upper right of picture), at Hopewell, New Jersey (group of buildings just above center). On May 12th, the decomposed body of the child was discovered in the woods (note automobiles parked on the road as it skirts the woods, left center), four miles from their home. For the next three years kidnaping became America's worst "racket," one sensational case following another. Public feeling eventually made possible the "Lindbergh Law," under which kidnaping, given certain circumstances, became a federal offense, punishable by death.

THE OLYMPIC GAMES

For the first time in history the Olympic Games were held in America in 1932. With impressive ceremonies Vice-President Charles Curtis opened the Olympiad in Los Angeles in an especially constructed stadium. Out of seventeen records established in the men's track and field events nine were made by United States entries. Most sensational were the victories in the 100-meter and 200-meter runs of the great Negro sprinter "Eddie" Tolan.

ATTEMPT ON ROOSEVELT'S LIFE

President-elect Roosevelt was in Miami on the night of February 15, 1933. The picture shows him as he waved to the welcoming crowd. A few seconds later, Joseph Zangara, a half-crazed person, fired at him, missing, but hitting Mayor Anton Cermak, of Chicago, who later died of the wound. Zangara paid for his crime with his life. The nation breathed relief at Roosevelt's escape for, aside from the horror of the crime itself, it was looking to him personally to lead the country out of the depression.

NAVAL REVIEW

In May, 1934, for the first time, the main fleet of the United States Navy passed through the Panama Canal from the Pacific to the Atlantic and proceeded northward to New York, where President Roosevelt, himself an enthusiastic sailor, and former Assistant Secretary of the Navy, reviewed it from the cruiser *Indianapolis* off Ambrose Light. It was the greatest concentration of American naval strength ever held. The country was vastly impressed, but the truth was that our fleet was both small and antiquated, and its air arm virtually non-existent. The United States was dangerously near to second-class naval status, and this in the face of a rapidly arming world. The renaissance of our Navy began under President Roosevelt, who managed to give the building of huge battleships a "help-employment" twist in 1936 when two battleships, two aircraft carriers, nine light cruisers, and more than thirty destroyers were laid down, partly with the normal naval appropriations of the year, partly with funds earmarked for unemployment work relief, but it was not until 1940 that the battleship *Washington,* first capital ship built in the country in nineteen years, was launched. In July of that year the President signed the two-ocean $4,000,000,000 Navy appropriation bill. The country, hoping that it was not too late, had subconsciously reconciled itself to participation in another world war but would not as yet admit in word or act the fact.

END OF AN ERA: DILLINGER'S LAST RIDE

In 1933 and 1934, in an effort to stem a tide of vicious but isolated crimes, the Federal government extended the police powers of its agents, and the "G" men commenced a war with gangdom. The turn of the tide came when John Dillinger, outstanding jail-breaker, bank-robber, and murderer, was cornered coming out of a Chicago theater, on July 22, 1934, and shot down by the Federal men. In the months following, the Federal agents, under the power given them, commenced to gain the upper hand. The era of the gangster was passing.

THE HAUPTMANN TRIAL

In September, 1934, two gasoline station attendants in the Bronx noticed a customer who paid them with a gold treasury note, then forbidden by Federal ruling. The result of their vigilance was the arrest of a German ex-convict, Bruno Richard Hauptmann, a Bronx carpenter, for the kidnapping and murder of the Lindbergh baby. Search of Hauptmann and his home resulted in the finding of $15,000 of the Lindbergh baby's ransom money, which had been paid by Colonel Lindbergh to the kidnaper, in a futile effort to regain the child. Placed on trial at Flemington, New Jersey, he was convicted and sentenced to death, in February, 1935.

THE SOCIAL SECURITIES ACT

By a vote of 372 to 33 the House of Representatives, on April 19, 1935, passed and sent to the Senate the Social Security Bill, levying wage taxes on industrial employers and workers to support a broad plan of old-age annuities and unemployment compensation. Based on an initial tax program of over $500,000,000 in 1937, the annuity reserve was calculated to reach nearly $33,000,000,000 by 1970. The bill was ratified by the Senate on August 9th, and the signature of the President on the 14th was acclaimed by more than 28,000,000 potential beneficiaries.

THE END OF A LOCAL DICTATORSHIP

As he walked from the State of Louisiana House of Representatives, a body which he completely dominated, United States Senator Huey P. Long was shot and fatally wounded on September 8, 1935, by Dr. Carl A. Weiss, who was the immediate recipient of sixty-one bullets from the guns of the State Police. Senator Long, a foe of the "New Deal", had developed a personal monarchy in his city and state that was nationally considered to be a menace to the principles of Democracy. He died September 10th, and was buried in the plaza of the State capitol at Baton Rouge. The picture shows the Senator entering the Canal Bank Building in New Orleans closely guarded by militia men.

WORLD WAR II IN THE MAKING

In 1936 Germany, under the leadership of madman Adolf Hitler and his Nazi party gangsters, began to show its claws. (Italy had invaded Ethiopia in 1935 with the consent of France's Laval.) The demilitarized Rhineland was reoccupied, and Hitler and Benito Mussolini, Italian Fascist leader, having signed a pact calling for a united front on all European problems, financed and promoted Francisco Franco of Spain in his successful fight to maintain his dictatorship. But the Spanish "show" was a rehearsal. On the sidelines, complacent, sat France, England, Russia, and the United States. The cause of the Spanish Revolution probably was done more harm than good in the popular mind here and in England by reason of its vigorous sponsorship by extreme leftwing groups, including the Communist party. The picture shows German transport detachments rumbling through the streets in front of Cologne Cathedral.

In 1937 Hitler repudiated the Versailles Treaty; in 1938 came Anschluss with Austria, the invasion of Czechoslovakia, and appeasement at Munich; and the Italian invasion of Albania followed in 1939. The world pot was coming to a boil very fast.

422

THE BOMBING OF THE *PANAY*

An unprovoked attack by Japanese fighting planes, culminating in the sinking of the United States gunboat *Panay* in the Yangtze River on the morning of December 12, 1937, and involving the death of one American and the wounding of fifteen, caused a serious break in U. S.–Japanese relationship. An immediate firm demand upon the Japanese Government for an accounting elicited a prompt apology and offer of reparation. Officially, the incident was closed with the receipt by the State Department of the Japanese agreement to reparation terms but throughout the country feeling, subsequently augmented by the exhibition of newsreels showing the actual bombing, ran so high that Japanese interests in the United States were seriously affected. The *Panay* bombing, subsequently known as the "so-sorry" incident, might have been a warning of things to come. The vessel had been the first command of Chester W. Nimitz, who in 1944 was Commander-in-Chief, Pacific Fleet.

RUSSO–GERMAN PACT

On August 23, 1939, the seemingly impossible happened and the shocked world was presented with the crowning glory of the Hitler-Von Ribbentrop (German Foreign Minister) foreign policy. The supposedly two most implacable enemies in the world suddenly proclaimed their unity in a pact binding each country to refrain from any act of force against the other and further binding each not to support warlike acts against either by a third power. Party lines did an about-face overnight. President Roosevelt hurriedly appealed for peace. But Hitler had assured himself against a war on two fronts. Many cried "Treachery!" but bungling western diplomacy had had much to do with the Nazi-Soviet *mariage de convenance*. The picture shows Stalin giving Joachim von Ribbentrop a jovial pat on the back as Soviet Foreign Minister Viachislav M. Molotov inspects a document providing for the partitioning of Poland. The German Fuehrer now turned westward to Holland, Belgium, France, and England. He was ready, at long last, for the war so carefully planned and, suiting his own time and convenience, he invaded Poland on September first. England and France, realizing they could remain aloof no longer, declared war on the third. Continuing as blind as Europe had been, the United States proclaimed its neutrality on the fifth and placed an embargo on arms shipments to all combatants.

424

BATTLE OF BRITAIN

The period September 1939 to April 1940 was known as the "phony war." France and England (and, remotely, the United States) felt safe behind the much-touted Maginot Line, but they had not counted on the new blitzkrieg tactics of the versatile German General Staff and the revival of the war of movement, made possible by the mechanization of whole armies, and the airplane. The spring of 1940 brought action. Denmark, Norway, Holland, Belgium, and France were invaded and conquered in rapid succession. "The hand that held the dagger has struck it into the back of its neighbor," said President Roosevelt as Mussolini, the jackal sensing the kill, declared war on prostrate France. A week previous the miracle of the evacuation of Dunkirk had been achieved by the British, and on June 17th France asked for an armistice. In August, Hitler decided England's time had come and there followed the Battle of Britain as the prelude to invasion. The average citizen suddenly found himself on the front lines. In the picture rescue workers, after sixteen hours, dig an aged man out of the wreckage of a London building. By November first Reich Marshal Hermann Goering's *Luftwaffe* had been defeated by the incredibly gallant and vastly outnumbered Royal Air Force. One in every five British homes had been damaged or destroyed, but the Germans had lost twenty-four hundred planes to less than a quarter of that number by the R.A.F. In the words of Prime Minister Winston Churchill, "Never in the field of human conflict was so much owed by so many to so few."

425

LONDON BURNS

The Germans were not slow in resorting to night bombing. There soon followed heavy raids on many English cities such as the devastating attack on Coventry in November. London, meanwhile, was a continuing target, and the destruction there reached its height with the big raid of December 29th in which the buildings in an enormous area in the heart of the city near famed St. Paul's Cathedral, here shown silhouetted in flame and smoke, were either blown to bits or disappeared in the fires that followed. Digging in the ruins, Britons vowed vengeance, no matter what the cost or the time required. Said Churchill, "I have nothing to offer but blood, toil, tears, and sweat." The events of May to December 1940 had shocked some but not all in the United States out of complacency and isolationism. France was gone. England seemed toppling. Were we next? The British people, now standing alone before the German military might, prepared for an invasion of their homeland.

PEACETIME DRAFT

An indication of how much sentiment in the United States had changed in a year was the passage by Congress of the Selective Training and Service Act, the first peacetime draft in the history of the country. Millions, however, still thought we could stay out of war and that the new army should be used only for defense. In October 1940, Secretary of War Henry L. Stimson drew the first number in the draft lottery. "One-five-eight," said President Roosevelt, and an armed force eventually to number eleven million men and women, more than twice the number in uniform in World War I, had been begun.

INDUCTION

Millions lined up at local draft boards. "No overseas service," cried the isolationists, but the young men in their hearts knew differently. Clerks, mechanics, soda jerkers, they faced the unpleasant job of soldiering—and of dying—realistically, even though part of the country did not. It was many months before the fresh troops had adequate equipment. The picture shows inductees crossing Park Avenue, N. Y., in the early hours of a winter morning.

427

LEND–LEASE

Gradually public sentiment was shifting, as illustrated by the President's trade, almost without protest, of fifty over-age destroyers to Britain in September 1940, in exchange for long leases on many naval and air bases in the Western Hemisphere. Later in the year the Administration proposed that the United States become the "arsenal of democracy" by building, lending, and leasing armaments of all kinds, as well as food and medical supplies, to the embattled British and their allies. In the picture Secretary of State Cordell Hull testifies for this Lend-Lease bill before the House Foreign Affairs Committee. The bill became law in March 1941, and by December 1, 1943, we had shipped $18,-609,000,000 worth of armaments and supplies to our Allies, including seven thousand planes, thirty-five hundred tanks, and a hundred and ninety-five thousand motor vehicles to Russia.

THIRD TERM

For the first time in its history the nation elected a man President for a third term in November 1940, and in the following January, Franklin Delano Roosevelt again repeated the solemn oath of office after Chief Justice Charles Evans Hughes. "Democracy is not dying," he declared. This unprecedented election was widely interpreted as a popular endorsement of the Administration's foreign policy by the general electorate. The envoys of Germany, Italy, and Japan attended the inauguration.

HOME DEFENSE

In May 1940, the President established the Office of Civilian Defense. Thousands of men and women enlisted as airplane spotters, air-raid wardens, civilian police, auxiliary firemen, and in many other jobs requiring long and tedious hours of volunteer service. The picture shows a mass meeting of wardens in San Francisco. Although the anticipated attack on the home front never materialized, the "CD" citizens performed valuable service not only in the abovementioned activities but as collectors of scrap metal, wastepaper, kitchen fats, and a host of other articles. Mayor Fiorello H. La Guardia of New York and Mrs. Eleanor R. Roosevelt, the President's wife, originally headed the OCD but later resigned after widespread popular criticism and were finally replaced by John B. Martin. In late May the President proclaimed an unlimited state of national emergency.

U.S. MARINES IN ICELAND

In order to prevent a German seizure and to keep the sea lanes open between the British Isles and the Western Hemisphere, Canadian troops occupied Iceland in the summer of 1940. Our forces later garrisoned the strategically important island, landing there for the first time in July 1941. Before the United States entered the war, American forces were on guard in Greenland, Dutch Guiana (Surinam) and in eight British outposts in the Western Hemisphere. Defense bases were leased to the U.S. at these British outposts in return for fifty outmoded U.S. destroyers, which were a welcome addition to the British navy in September 1940, when the exchange was effected. The picture shows a small American contingent somewhere in Iceland in 1942, in front of their prefabricated barracks which skilled American labor manufactured in an unprecedentedly short time, and which soon after Pearl Harbor dotted the countrysides of many nations.

PHOTO BY U.S. ARMY SIGNAL CORPS.

A HOUSE DIVIDED

Up till the moment of Pearl Harbor a sharp division continued within the country as to whether we could or could not avoid actual war. The isolationist issue cut across party lines, as exemplified by the fact that Wendell Willkie, defeated Republican Presidential candidate, was one of the country's leading advocates of the Roosevelt foreign policy. Many groups were bitterly opposed, especially the America First Committee and large sections in the great Middle West for whom the Chicago *Tribune* pretended to speak. Here Charles Lindbergh speaks to an overflow crowd of twenty thousand at Madison Square Garden in New York, just five weeks before Pearl Harbor. Less influential but more noisy were such outright pro-German and anti-semitic groups as Father Coughlin's Social Justice, the Silver Shirts, the Christian Front, the Christian Mobilizers, the Bunds, and others of the "lunatic fringe."

ATLANTIC CHARTER

In a history-making conference held in mid-Atlantic in August 1941, the two leaders of the English-speaking peoples drafted the "Atlantic Charter." Drawing up a plan for maintenance of peace after the aggressor nations shall have been defeated, the statesmen proposed to establish ". . . a peace which will afford to all nations the means of dwelling in safety within their own boundaries, and which will afford assurance that all men in all the lands may live out their lives in freedom from fear and want." The Charter declared against territorial aggrandizement, for the right of all peoples to choose their own form of government, for the right of access for all to the world's trade and raw materials, for freedom of the seas, and for the disarmament of the aggressor nations. Just two months previously Hitler, tossing overboard his pact with the Soviets, had invaded Russia.

ACME PHOTO.

LABOR TROUBLES

Strikes were not too frequent in the early days of the national emergency, but as the cost of living rose and as the Administration sought to freeze wages under the Little Steel formula labor disputes increased, and they continued to plague the country throughout the war period, the Army being forced to take over even the nation's railroads in December 1943. Among the troops, resentment over the situation on the home front was widespread. Typical of the early troubles was the wild-cat strike at North American Aviation, Inc., Inglewood, California, in October 1941, when the Army took over, on the President's order, this vitally important defense plant.

434

PEARL HARBOR

The end of national disunity and a twenty-year attempt to live with our head in the sand came to a sudden end on the quiet Sunday morning of December 7, 1941, at our great Pearl Harbor naval base in the Hawaiian Islands. While their envoys lulled us at Washington with words of peace Japanese level and dive bombers and torpedo planes struck. The attack was masterfully planned. Of the eight battleships we had in the Pacific Ocean on that morning eight were hit, four were sunk. The damage was enormous. Thirty-three hundred soldiers, sailors, and Marines died, but the attack, designed to knock us out of the war before we had begun to fight, failed in its objective. However, Admiral Husband E. Kimmel, Commander-in-Chief of the Fleet, who had been at Pearl Harbor, and Lieutenant General Walter C. Short, Commander of the Hawaiian Department, were relieved of their posts and trials by court-martial were ordered for them after a five-man board, headed by Supreme Court Justice Owen J. Roberts, had made its report. The board said that the Jap success was due principally to the dereliction of duty of these two officers, but the facts are yet to be determined. The picture shows the sinking of the *Arizona* after being blasted by bombs. In the face of the disaster the nation united overnight, and in a few days we had declared war on Japan, Germany, and Italy.

PHOTOS BY U.S. ARMY SIGNAL CORPS.

LOSS OF THE PHILIPPINES

Soon after the Pearl Harbor attack came Japanese assaults on Hong Kong, Singapore, Guam, Wake, and the Philippines. All fought back bravely but unsuccessfully. The heroic resistance of the American and native troops became, however, a national symbol. The picture shows men of an anti-tank company defending their positions on Bataan where 36,000 men, "due to complete physical exhaustion," were forced to surrender on April 9th. Almost the sole bright spot for the Allies throughout the winter and spring (the British were retreating in North Africa) was the vigorous offensive of the Russian armies on the Eastern Front.

GENERAL DOUGLAS MacARTHUR

Former chief-of-staff of the U.S. Army, Gen. MacArthur was organizer of the defense of the Philippines, where he commanded the American and Filipino army until March 1942, when he became chief of United Nations forces in the western Pacific theatre of the war with headquarters in Australia. He was succeeded in the Philippines by Lieut. General Jonathan M. Wainwright.

436

TOKYO RAID

National morale received a much-needed lift with the announcement that a daylight air raid had been made on Japan's capital, as well as on Yokohama, Nagoya, and Kobe on April 18, 1942. It was a combined operation of the Army and Navy, planned for months, and led by Admiral William F. Halsey, Jr., and Brigadier General James H. Doolittle. Protected by Navy fliers from the carrier *Enterprise* and an accompanying task force, the Army bombers took off from the *Hornet* 850 miles from Japan. Here Doolittle's plane leaves the carrier, which was later sunk at Santa Cruz. The bombing was at very low altitudes and extremely accurate. The raid was a harbinger of things to come as were others, notably those on the Marcus and Makin Islands. "Remember Pearl Harbor!" was a national cry, but behind the holding battles of 1942 we secured our supply lines around the world, organized our strength, and quickly, but with an efficiency never equaled in the world before, prepared to take the offensive.

SUBMARINE SINKINGS

The Battle of the Atlantic was perhaps the greatest victory won by the Allies in 1942. In 1917 the German U-boats had almost starved England. In 1942 they were at it again, greatly increased in numbers and employing new techniques. Men and goods had to be safely transported to Russia, England, and the Middle East. It wasn't until the fall of the year that the British and American navies felt they had turned the tide. Destroyers bore the brunt of the protective work, assisted more and more by the new destroyer escorts, landbased airplanes, and planes from midget carriers converted from merchant vessels. But the submarines, frequently operating in packs, took a terrific toll, almost six hundred vessels being sunk by the end of the year. Early in 1944 the Navy announced that loss of ships due to submarine action had been reduced by 60% in 1943, as against the previous year, and that about two hundred U-boats had been sunk in the Atlantic in the past twelve months. The picture shows part of a convoy photographed from a protecting British plane.

HISTORIC MIDWAY

History will undoubtedly put down the Battle of Midway, June 3–6, 1942, as one of the decisive battles of the world. It came as a result of Japan's attempt to break through the iron circle that was slowly being forged around her stolen empire. Because of it the initiative on land and sea in the Pacific passed into our hands and the importance of the Japanese landings in the Aleutian Islands was nullified. Japan had made a previous attempt to break the iron ring in the Battle of the Coral Sea in May, and it had been in part an enemy victory. Midway followed soon after. The enemy fleet was impressive—the largest of the war. Brilliantly fought, it was a complete American victory, despite the loss of the gallant *Yorktown,* and cost the Japanese four carriers sunk, two cruisers sunk (the picture shows one of the Mogami class after being hit) and three others damaged, three battleships damaged, one severely, one light cruiser damaged, three or four destroyers sunk, and three transports and cargo ships hit. With his ships went Hirohito's dream of world empire. Said Admiral Chester W. Nimitz, ". . . our citizens can now rejoice that a momentous victory is in the making. . . . Pearl Harbor has now been partially avenged. Vengeance will not be complete until Japanese sea power has been reduced to impotence. . . . Perhaps we will be forgiven if we claim we are about midway to our objective."

439

MARINES AT GUADALCANAL

August 7, 1942, marked our first major offensive. Guadalcanal and near-by islands in the central Solomons were the objectives. The campaign began with a naval defeat off Savo Island and ended with another naval action off Tassafaronga on December first, but the Marines, those toughest of fighters, led by Major General Alexander A. Vandegrift, established and held their beachheads and finally wiped out the Japanese. The top picture shows a hangar at hard-won Henderson Field burning after a Japanese attack and in the bottom are Marines firing an 155-mm. howitzer. Innumerable enemy attempts to reinforce the island during the campaign were repulsed. Winning the island cost many ships and men, but the victory secured our supply lines and our military men declared it worth the price. The action at Tassafaronga marked the last attempt of the Japanese to relieve their forces on Guadalcanal. The leathernecks were fast making a lot of bad Japs into good ones. The closing months of 1942 saw the Allies turn from retreat and defense to the attack, in the Pacific, in Russia with the lifting of the siege of Stalingrad, in Egypt with the British 8th Army's attack at El Alamein, and in West Africa with the landings of the British and Americans in Morocco and Algeria.

440

AFRICAN INVASION

For three years the British and the Germans had fought a seesaw battle over the sands of North Africa, but in October 1942, Lieutenant General Bernard L. Montgomery, leading the famous 8th Army, was ready at last to destroy Marshal Rommel's Afrika Korps and he attacked from the El Alamein Line, deep in Egypt. On November 7th the world was startled by the news of American and British landings in Algeria and Morocco. This African invasion was led by an American, Lieutenant General Dwight D. Eisenhower. Here Americans, with the flag in the lead, swim ashore from landing boats at Surcouf and debark from a large transport at Casablanca. The Allies now pressed eastward while Montgomery pursued the fleeing Rommel westward through Libya and into Tunisia, where in May 1943, near Tunis and Bizerte, his army was destroyed. The capture of Tunisia had taken longer than expected, and Rommel himself had escaped to fight another day, but the Mediterranean was now secure; supply lines were shortened by thousands of miles, and Europe's southern coast was open to attack.

441

SICILIAN AND ITALIAN INVASIONS

The vast armada of 3000 ships, 160,000 men, 14,000 vehicles, 600 tanks, and 1800 guns which sailed for Sicily in early July was greater than the original African landing force. The picture shows invasion boats at a North African port ready for the jump across the Mediterranean. The Germans fought fiercely, especially against the British at Catania, but the island fell in mid-August, and a month later we were in Italy itself and on the road to Rome. Impossible weather conditions and mountainous terrain slowed the advance north of Naples in early 1944. Meantime, the jackal Mussolini had resigned; Italy had surrendered; most of the Italian fleet had escaped to Malta; and the nation, under Marshal Pietro Badoglio, had declared war against its former partner. Most important result of the Italian landing was the acquisition of airfields on the continent for the future bombing of Germany.

442

BOMBING FORTRESS EUROPE

By early 1943 the R.A.F. began the long-awaited major attack by air on Europe. Later in the year the United States 8th Air Force was itself able to put 1500 planes in a day into the air. Mainly, the British bombed by night, the Americans by daylight and at higher altitudes. Example—in the heaviest raid on London the *Luftwaffe* dropped 450 tons of bombs, but in one raid on Dusseldorf the R.A.F. dropped 2000 tons, and such raids became almost daily occurrences. The British were paying back with interest. After it was announced that Hamburg as a city had ceased to exist and that the Battle of the Ruhr was won and its industries knocked out, the British and Americans turned on Berlin. By mid-1944 Hitler's capital, over which Goering had promised enemy planes would never fly, was destroyed and the government moved elsewhere. Here Flying Fortresses of the 8th Air Force Bomber Command turn away from the Focke-Wulf aircraft plant at Marienburg as smoke rises from the target.

FIRST STEPS BACK IN THE PACIFIC

In 1943 not much actual land was taken back from the Japanese, but the Americans improved their strategic position on all fronts. First the enemy was pushed out of the Aleutians and the Solomons. Next General MacArthur began his drive in the south and southwest, and we landed in the Marshall, Caroline, and Gilbert Islands and made advances on New Guinea and New Britain. The Allied commanders made it clear, however, that the decisive drives must wait the end of European hostilities. Whenever it got the chance (and it got it less and less often, for the Japanese showed an increasing reluctance to fight at sea) the Navy inflicted the heaviest sort of damage on the enemy fleet. Figures were not official, but at least ten cruisers, eleven destroyers, and many other warships were sunk, an equal number, and perhaps more, seriously damaged, and dozens of troopships and freighters sent to the bottom. Our airmen gained complete control of the skies in every American offensive. In the remarkable action picture at the top, at the height of the battle for Tarawa, ("the bloodiest in Marine Corps history") Marines plunge over a palm-log wall. In the lower picture Marines, tired, dirty, and unshaven, plod out of the jungle after the action at Tarakina Point, near Bougainville, New Guinea, where they met their fiercest opposition.

444

PAN–AMERICAN DEFENSE CONFERENCE HELD AT RIO DE JANEIRO

Under Secretary of State Sumner Welles, head of the United States' delegation to the Inter-American Conference which met in January 1942, waves his hat in response to cheers from spectators as he arrives at the opening session of the meeting. Representatives of the twenty-one American republics mapped the policy to be followed now that the war had spread to the Western Hemisphere; most of the Latin American countries severed relations with the Axis powers soon afterwards. Another outcome of the discussions held by the American ministers of foreign affairs was the meeting of military and naval experts of the American governments at Washington, March 30, 1942, to study and recommend measures necessary for the defense of the two continents.

PHOTOGRAPH FROM WIDE WORLD PHOTOS, INC.

RATIONING

As the nation got under way with the job of supplying troops spread over every continent in the world and with the feeding of many civilian populations, the people at home tightened their belts. By Presidential Order the Office of Price Administration had been established in April 1941. Such articles as automobiles, tires, typewriters, radios, refrigerators, and a host of metal goods disappeared completely from the nation's stores, and items such as sugar, coffee, gasoline, meat, canned goods, heating oil, coal, and shoes were more or less severely rationed. The picture shows New Yorkers registering for gas-ration cards at a public school. As was to be expected, grumbling and sharp criticism of the OPA developed, but saner heads reflected that the United States, even at war, was still able to maintain the highest standard of living, and of luxury, of any nation in the world—and were thankful.

AMERICAN INDUSTRY

Production rates achieved by American industry in the war years were staggering in size. The Federal Government spent more money on the war in the one year 1943 than it had spent in the first 150 years of its existence, including all World War I expenditures. Some items were produced in 1943 at twenty-five times the 1941 rate. Example—the nation constructed about 1,100,000 tons of shipping in 1941. The President called for 8,000,000 deadweight tons of merchant shipping in 1942 and 16,000,000 in 1943. Actually we produced 8,400,000 in 1942 and 19,200,000 in 1943 and, by the end of that year, had attained a 25,000,000-tons-a-year rate of construction. The picture is of several of the ways at the famed Kaiser shipyards at Vancouver, Washington. Seven vessels can be seen. Articles of all sorts, down to the humblest, were produced for ourselves and our Allies in quantities thought impossible before the war. American capital and labor, but above all American inventiveness and resourcefulness, were responsible. Marshal Stalin of Russia, a man not given to many words, paid tribute to our production at the Teheran Conference in late 1943 when he admitted that without our supplies Russia's great offensive then just entering Poland would have been impossible.

THE TURBULENT HOME FRONT

The dark side of our war effort was on the home front. Undoubtedly the people were behind the war to a finish, but well-organized groups continued to fight for their selfish interests to the nation's cost. This condition was especially dangerous since the real battles were yet to begin for us. The farmers wrecked a subsidy plan for keeping down the cost of living; industry refused to renegotiate war contracts; Congress refused to tax war-swollen incomes; certain groups continued to undermine faith in our allies, Great Britain and Russia, and, most dangerous of all, labor, grown powerful after ten years of having its own way, embarked on a series of disastrous strikes (the coal miners, for instance, walking out for the fourth time) which slowed production and drove wages upward. Here workers check in their equipment at a mine in Ohio as they respond to strike orders from their leader, John L. Lewis. The home front seemed in danger of falling apart.

THE TEHERAN CONFERENCE

In late 1943 there took place in Teheran in Iran the most momentous gathering of political leaders the world had seen since the Versailles conference. Hitler and Mussolini had never staged anything to equal it. Prime Minister Churchill and President Roosevelt had met often and in many places, but Marshal Stalin, whose victorious armies were just then nearing the old Polish border, had held aloof. In the picture Marshal Stalin, in trim new uniform, rises to greet Sarah Churchill, the Prime Minister's daughter. Roosevelt and Churchill had proceeded to the meeting after completing a previous one with Generalissimo Chiang Kai-shek at which the war in China and in the Pacific was discussed. At Teheran not only were plans agreed on for the final crushing of Germany, but talks were begun on problems of the peace. Said a communiqué, "No power can prevent our destroying the German armies by land, their U-boats by sea, and their war plants from the air." The Allies stood poised for the greatest military operation in history, the invasion of northern Europe.

449

GENERAL MARSHALL

Commander of the largest Army in ou[r]
history and the second largest in worl[d]
history (Russia's is larger) is General o[f]
the Armies George C. Marshall—re[-]
served, blunt, democratic, even-tempered
and fatalistic. His achievement is that h[e]
not only raised this Army in a democrati[c]
country, at times at war with itself, bu[t]
subsequently deployed it over six conti[-]
nents. In addition he met and placated o[r]
defeated the home-front politicians. N[o]
other Chief of Staff has combined suc[h]
qualities, and for this his fame will prob[-]
ably outlive those of his predecessors i[n]
office in other wars.

GENERAL ARNOLD

Sidetracked to a quiet post after he defended "Billy" Mitchell in 1925, General Henry Harley Arnold now commands the biggest air force in world history. Nineteen forty-four, with 2,500,-
000 officers and men and 100,000 airplanes under his command, will tell his
story. Aviation, and what it can accom-
plish in peace and war, has been his great
devotion since he learned to fly with the
Wright brothers in 1911. He, together
with Lieutenant General Ira C. Eaker,
commander of the 8th Air Force in England, are the great champions of high-
altitude daylight bombing. He's known
as a tough officer but one given to sudden
streaks of kindliness.

450

GENERAL EISENHOWER

The man who commands all Allied forces in the European theater, General Dwight David Eisenhower, has won the respect not only of those under him but of the political leaders, notably Prime Minister Churchill. His success in establishing a true "fighting partnership" between the British and Americans was one reason why he was first given the command in Africa and then in England. The other reason is his ability as a fighting man. He leads the greatest invasion in history. In his previous Army life he specialized in tanks and airplanes. He is inquisitive, a hard worker, and tremendously friendly.

451

GENERAL MacARTHUR

General Douglas MacArthur was, in early 1944, undoubtedly a very great general but with his big victories still unwon. His defeat at Bataan burns deep within him and will not be exorcised until the Japanese are finally smashed. It is a cult, almost a religion, and he nourishes it while he waits for his great chance. Since his watchword as a soldier is "Attack! Attack!" he undoubtedly waits impatiently. He had hoped to be on his way long since. He is aloof, pious, epigrammatic in speech, and a great showman, the latter quality being one that he shares with such military leaders as Caesar and Napoleon.

ADMIRAL KING

The great asset of Admiral of the Fleet Ernest J. King, commander of every American warship, officer, bluejacket, and Marine, is that he knows surface craft, submarines, and aircraft, all from personal experience. Physically, he is tall, thin, and straight; mentally, he is hot-tempered, stern, formal to the point of ceremoniousness, and just. He has been described as a "thinking machine of brilliant, ice-cold clarity." He plans every major move made by the Navy, and although the initiative is his, he believes in telling subordinates what to do, not how to do it. The latter is their job.

ADMIRAL LEAHY

In the days of peace, between the two wars, Admiral William D. Leahy played a larger part than any other man in deciding our Naval policies. In 1940, President Roosevelt sent him to Vichy to help Pétain resist collaboration. It was an impossibly difficult job. On his return the President appointed him Chief of Staff. In this spot he helps direct the affairs of the world's largest and most powerful fleet. He had much to do with building our chain of Caribbean defense ports, now so formidable that no enemy would dare attack us on the Atlantic side without first reducing them. He is strict on duty but friendly and informal off it.

452

ADMIRAL NIMITZ

The man in charge of the largest battle area in United States naval history, the man directly responsible for virtually every major naval offensive against the Japanese, is Admiral Chester W. Nimitz. His distinguishing quality is calmness. For months after Pearl Harbor the country impatiently asked, "Where's the fleet?" Nimitz kept silent. Finally came his answer—Midway. He had destroyed one of the greatest invasion armadas of all time and turned the tide. Not by any means to be underestimated has been his steady whittling down of the Japanese fleet. His specialty is the submarine, and about their activities he has been most silent.

453

ADMIRAL HALSEY

We have always loved a tough-talking naval officer. Such a one is Admiral William F. Halsey. He's unique in that he was the fifth four-star admiral appointed, whereas tradition calls for no more than four four-star men on active duty at one time. He commands the South Pacific area and forces and, as such, has borne the brunt of the combat responsibility since late 1942. Already he has exploded the myth of Japanese invincibility. His men love him. Even down to his tattooing, he's a gruff sea dog who hates spit and polish and publicity, but who hates, and has always hated above all else, the Japs.

SYNTHETIC QUININE

No chemical discovery has had wider military and social significance than that of synthetic quinine. Every year, before the war, three million people died of malaria. The only effective preventative and cure for malaria was quinine, which was obtained from the chinchona groves of Java. In 1944, with the source of supply entirely in enemy hands, and with malaria spreading because of war migrations, this mosquito-borne disease threatened to become a world menace. Atabrine and other substitutes were not able to take the place of quinine itself.

In May of 1944 the two young scientists shown here, Robert B. Woodward, 26 (left), and William E. Doering, 27, working in the laboratories of Harvard University, succeeded in producing synthetic quinine from toluol and acetylene, both of which can be derived from coal or petroleum. Government agencies immediately set about translating the Woodward-Doering process into large-scale production.

453–a

SUPERFORTRESS

America's super-bomber, the Boeing B-29 Superfortress, made its first public appearance early in June, 1944, in a spectacular raid on the war industries of Japan. The B-29 carries a larger bomb load, has greater range, higher speed, and service altitude than any other bomber in the world. It is half again as large as the Flying Fortress. Its engines are approximately twice as powerful. It is nearly one hundred feet long. Its wing spread is one hundred and forty-one feet. Its armament includes an unspecified number of 50-caliber machine guns and a 20 mm. cannon, all electrically aimed and fired. Its speed, while still a military secret, is known to compare favorably with the fastest fighter planes. Here two of the mighty ships are shown in flight with a Flying Fortress.

The new plane embodies the most outstanding and daring aerodynamic developments and ideas gained in combat experience in the war. Army Air Force Materiel Command technicians, the Army Air Force General Staff and operating commands, as well as Boeing engineers, coordinated their efforts to produce this new weapon.

453–b

REPUBLICAN CONVENTION

Thomas E. Dewey, Michigan-born, racket-busting Governor of New York, was chosen by the 1944 Republican National Convention as its presidential candidate to meet the fourth term drive of Franklin D. Roosevelt. Governor John W. Bricker, of Ohio, won the Republican nomination for Vice-President. In the jam-packed Chicago stadium, in which the convention was held, Dewey was nominated by a count of 1056 votes to 1. The sole opposition ballot was cast for General Douglas MacArthur. The Republicans seemed to have their best chance, because of wide-spread dissatisfaction over Washington's management of domestic affairs, to defeat President Roosevelt since 1932. Both sides admitted, however, that the course of the war during the summer and early fall would have a real effect on the November vote.

453–c

FALL OF ROME

At high noon, June 5, 1944, Allied Headquarters officially announced the occupation of the Eternal City, first Axis capital to be knocked out of the war. Later that day Lieutenant General Mark W. Clark, commander of the 5th Army of the United States, met his corps commanders on a balcony in the city, and announced, "We have smashed parts of the German 10th Army which faced us in the south. We are well across the Tiber." Here, in his three-star jeep, he stops to chat with a priest of the Vatican staff.

Meanwhile, fighter-bombers hammered away at the fleeing German columns, now in fast retreat to a new defense line supposed to be based on Pisa, Florence, and Ravenna. Technically, German Field Marshal "Smiling Albert" Kesselring's forces had been battered out of Rome on Trinity Sunday, the day before. Through the din of battle the United States and Canadian troops could hear church bells, summoning the faithful to mass. Twenty-four hours after Rome's capitulation was official, King Vittorio Emanuele turned over his powers to his son, 36-year-old Crown Prince Umberto.

453–d

INVASION OF SAIPAN

The Allied squeeze-play against Japan proper took a decisive turn, early in June, 1944, when United States troops made a surprise landing on Saipan, one of the Mariana Islands. This marked the first direct Allied invasion of territory belonging to Japan prior to the outbreak of war. At Saipan the Second and Fourth Marine Divisions, conquerors of Tarawa, Roi, and Naumur were in action, plus the Army's Twenty-seventh Division, mostly New Yorkers. It was the bloodiest and most costly fighting since Tarawa. Navy guns had covered their landings but the island was too mountainous for either naval guns or air bombing to be of much effect after the initial stages. Nevertheless, the Japs, abandoned by their own defeated naval rescue forces, were cut off. They soon burrowed into the central uplands, leaving the southwestern end of the island to the Americans. In a two-week's land and sea fight the Japanese lost thirty capital ships, thirteen landing barges packed with reinforcements, and 757 aircraft. Early in July the island, with its airfields within bombing range of Tokyo, fell. The first slice of the Japanese Empire had been cut.

Here, men aboard a carrier cheer as a blazing enemy aircraft plunges into the sea during a preliminary raid on Saipan in February in which the Japs lost one hundred and thirty-five planes.

453–e

INVASION

The long-awaited invasion of "Fortress Europe" from the north began at six o'clock on the morning of June 6, 1944. The Allies crossed the English Channel in approximately 4000 ships. Escorting the troop transports were twelve battleships, eighty destroyers, and 7500 planes. Four airborne divisions and two parachute divisions went overhead. In the greatest military gamble in history, the Allied troops soon were holding beachheads along a ninety mile stretch of the Norman coast from the mouth of the Seine to Barfleur, near Cherbourg. Here are shown American troops hurrying ashore.

The Germans were apparently caught napping. The Allies had expected to lose ten per cent of their landing craft. Instead they got through virtually intact. Closely timed bombardment by warships and planes put enough coast defense guns out of action to make landings possible in most places without serious casualties.

453–f

CLEANING UP

General Eisenhower, from headquarters in England, commanded the mighty assault on Europe, while General Sir Bernard Law Montgomery, hero of the North African campaign, opposed his old foe Marshal Rommel on the scene of the fighting. Major General Omar N. Bradley commanded the Americans who immediately set about cutting off the Cherbourg peninsula, while against veteran German troops the British held the vital opposite flank, and later captured Caen. The Americans were back in France for the first time since World War I and the British for the first time since their evacuation of Dunkirk in 1940. They were making good their promise to Hitler to return and even the score. Here American engineers rapidly clear the main street of St. Sauveur for traffic after the town was taken during the drive for Cherbourg.

453—g

CHERBOURG FALLS

Cherbourg, France's third largest port, and its first strategic city to fall into Allied hands, capitulated to the American invasion forces on June 27th, three weeks after the storming of the Normandy beaches. Six hours later, Major General Joseph Lawton Collins, American commander of the forces that stormed Cherbourg, in an official ceremony returned the city to French hands. The Germans lost 30,000 troops. The Allies gained one of the best commercial seaports on the continent. Convoys may now steam directly there from United States ports. In the picture Lieutenant General Carl Wilhelm von Schlieben, in helmet center background, commander of the Cherbourg garrison, and Rear Admiral Walter Heunecke, in center with long coat, commander of the Normandy area, emerge from their cave headquarters to surrender to American troops under the protection of the traditional white flag.

GEORGE WASHINGTON
1732–1799, PRESIDENT, 1789–1797

"If you speak of solid information and sound judgment," said Patrick Henry at the First Continental Congress, "Colonel Washington is unquestionably the greatest man on the floor." Unanimously elected Commander-in-Chief of the Revolutionary forces, Washington led them to victory and was afterwards unanimously elected President of the nation. A large man, six feet two in height and more than two hundred pounds in weight, he was one of the country's richest men. His two terms were most important since the prestige of his great name held in check many internal wrangles during the early years and so allowed the young country to begin its life on a safe but enlightened basis.

JOHN ADAMS
1735–1826, PRESIDENT, 1797–1801

Two great issues marked the administration of John Adams. His Vice-President was Thomas Jefferson, a man whose political faith opposed the President's on all counts. First, Adams and the New Englanders were strongly against Western expansion while Jefferson as strongly favored it. Second, Adams was a Federalist fighting for a government "by an aristocracy of talents and wealth," but Jefferson placed his faith in the common people. The times were not harmonious. He was the first President to live in the White House. The old rivals, Adams and Jefferson, died on the same day but, unaware of the passing of his opponent, Adams' last words were, "Jefferson still survives."

454

JAMES MADISON

1751–1836, PRESIDENT, 1809–1817

Secretary of State under Jefferson, it was the latter's wish that Madison succeed him. He was rightly called the Father of the Constitution because of his vigorous defense of and fight for its adoption. One of the ablest men of his day, he lacked the gift of winning the affection of the people, and his greatest asset as a politician was his charming wife, "Dolly." He saw the country safely through the War of 1812, for which it was completely unprepared, but at one point his popularity sank dangerously low because of consistent military defeats. The war, in which for the last time the continental United States was invaded, taught Americans the importance of national defense and a strong Navy.

THOMAS JEFFERSON

1743–1826, PRESIDENT, 1801–1809

Before his death the Sage of Monticello wrote an inscription for his tomb setting forth what he felt were his three chief claims to remembrance: "Here was buried Thomas Jefferson, author of the Declaration of American Independence, of the Statute of Virginia for Religious Freedom, and Father of the University of Virginia." At least equal in importance was his influence in turning the United States to popular rather than aristocratic democracy, his successful struggle against Aaron Burr, and his negotiation of the Louisiana Purchase by which we acquired for future expansion the tremendously rich territory of almost all of thirteen future states. He was the founder of the Democratic party.

455

JAMES MONROE

1758–1831, PRESIDENT, 1817–1825

Harmony followed the close of the War of 1812, and the eight years of Monroe's administration are still cited as "the era of good feeling." It was a time of expansion and of prosperity. Five states were admitted to the Union; Florida was purchased from Spain, and Europe was warned to keep hands off American and Pan-American affairs in the Monroe Doctrine. This policy has greatly influenced our foreign affairs for well over a century. Even the question of slavery was momentarily and peacefully settled by the Missouri Compromise of 1820. Not a great statesman, Monroe had, in the words of John Adams, "a mind . . . sound in its ultimate judgments, and firm in its final conclusions."

JOHN QUINCY ADAMS

1767–1848, PRESIDENT, 1825–1829

Son of the second President, John Quincy Adams was elected to office in one of the bitterest campaigns ever waged in this country. The Fathers of the Revolution were too old to serve, and for the first time the Republic looked to a new generation. Under him sectionalism rapidly developed. Main issue was the tariff which Adams, a New Englander and an opponent of Jefferson's theory of states' rights, favored. During his administration John C. Calhoun developed the famous theory of nullification—the Federal Government was the agency of the states, the Constitution was the states' book of instructions, and the states should determine when these instructions had been violated.

456

MARTIN VAN BUREN

1782–1862, PRESIDENT, 1837–1841

Van Buren, hand-picked by Jackson, who completely dominated his party, was the first President born an American citizen. He was an adroit politician, long a leader of the notorious Albany Regency which controlled politics in New York State. The important event of his administration, and in large measure the cause of his defeat when he ran for a second term in office, was the Panic of 1837. His party had failed to find any remedy for the general era of "bad times." The period had been brought on by over-speculation in the newly opened Western areas where railroads were being built and where immigrants were buying land at ever-rising prices. It was the nation's first great financial crisis.

ANDREW JACKSON

1767–1845, PRESIDENT, 1829–1837

Son of the frontier, hero of the Battle of New Orleans and the Indian wars, "Old Hickory" was the first man of the common people to become President. As such, it was strange that he was the first to build up a political machine, including the "spoils system," and first to introduce patronage into national politics. No American has left a stronger mark on our political system. His headstrong temperament filled his terms with quarrels, the two greatest of which he won, the first when he forced Calhoun to compromise his doctrine of nullification, the second when, representing the popular will, he destroyed the Bank of the United States and defeated its president, Nicholas Biddle.

WILLIAM HENRY HARRISON
1773–1841, PRESIDENT, MARCH 4–APRIL 4, 1841

The Whigs selected General William Henry (Tippecanoe) Harrison, an old hero of the Indian wars, as their candidate in 1840, and, taking a leaf from the book of the Democrats, rushed him into office with a campaign emphasizing his homespun virtues and simplicity in contrast with the supposedly luxurious lives of such Democrats as Van Buren. This was the famous "log-cabin-and-cider" campaign, so called because the General was born in a log cabin and served cider at his table instead of wine. The tumult and the shouting were too much for the old man. Overrun by hordes of Whigs seeking office after twelve years of political starvation, he fell ill with pneumonia and died.

JOHN TYLER
1790–1862, PRESIDENT, 1841–1845

The tenth President was the first to reach office because of another's death. His had been a political choice, for he was an embittered Democrat nominated by the Whigs to catch the votes of his former party under the slogan, "Tippecanoe and Tyler too." Thus he led a party that opposed him and whose real head was Henry Clay, who finally had the Whigs declare that "all political connection between them and John Tyler was at an end." In the election of 1844 he was side-tracked by the Whigs who nominated Clay unanimously to run against the Democrat Polk. In 1861 he was made a member of the Confederate Congress, but he died at Richmond before he had a chance to serve.

458

ZACHARY TAYLOR

1784–1850, PRESIDENT, 1849–JULY 9, 1850

For forty years a soldier, with a term of service extending from the War of 1812 to the war with Mexico, General Zachary Taylor came to the Presidency without political experience of any kind. The Whigs nominated him because they had learned that the easiest way to beat the Democrats was to select a popular military figure; after the war with Mexico old "Rough and Ready" was the best-qualified man in the country in this respect. During his term of office the slavery controversy grew sharper and sharper as the country and its great orators Clay, Calhoun, and Webster debated the issue. Taylor, as a soldier, favored enforcement of authority and talk of secession moved him to anger.

JAMES KNOX POLK

1795–1849, PRESIDENT, 1845–1849

In 1844 the Whigs ran Henry Clay against a young lawyer from Tennessee, one James K. Polk (originally Pollock), and lost the election. Polk's administration was notable for the lowering of the tariff laws, acquisition of Texas, California, and New Mexico through the war with Mexico, and for the final settlement of the boundary dispute (Fifty-four Forty or Fight) with Great Britain over the limits of the Oregon Territory. Polk declared himself for the masses and condemned the Whigs and the Federalists for trying to transfer money "from the pockets of the people to the favored classes." It is interesting to note that Mrs. Polk banished dancing and drinking from White House receptions.

459

MILLARD FILLMORE
1800–1874, PRESIDENT, 1850–1853

The thirteenth President was a man of many virtues who would probably never have reached national distinction except for the accident of General Taylor's death which raised him from the Vice-Presidency to the highest office. He was an earnest, self-made man, a lawyer, eminent "for his calm and pacific temperament." Conservative by nature, he sought to enforce the great Compromise of 1850 which had been Clay's handiwork, but he wrecked his political career in 1852 when he signed the Fugitive Slave Law providing for the surrender of runaway slaves. This law probably had as much to do with bringing on the Civil War as the controversy over slavery in the territories.

FRANKLIN PIERCE
1804–1869, PRESIDENT, 1853–1857

The Whig formula for winning the Presidency with a military candidate met defeat in 1852 when Franklin Pierce, a New Hampshire Democrat, won a smashing victory over General Winfield Scott with a platform advocating slavery and tariff for revenue only. The Whig party did not survive the disaster. Pierce selected an able Cabinet, including men of all factions, Northern and Southern Democrats, anti-slavery Northerners, a Massachusetts Whig, and an ardent states' rights Southerner, Jefferson Davis. He was, however, no man to guide the country through the brewing storm. Clay, Calhoun, and Webster, who preferred compromise to disunion, were dead. Young radicals were in control.

460

ABRAHAM LINCOLN

1809–1865, PRESIDENT, 1861–1865

"A homely hero born of star and sod," the son of Thomas Lincoln and Nancy Hanks was at the beginning of his career dismissed as "an ignorant Western boor," yet he alone among the Presidents holds an unquestioned position at the side of George Washington. His tragic death on April 15, 1865, at the hands of John Wilkes Booth added a martyr's crown to his glories, but his place among the immortals was already secure. The feeling of the people is truly recorded in the inscription behind his statue in the great Lincoln Memorial in Washington: "In this temple as in the hearts of the people for whom he saved the Union the memory of Abraham Lincoln is enshrined forever."

461

JAMES BUCHANAN

1791–1868, PRESIDENT, 1857–1861

Having won distinction in both houses of Congress as a diplomatic representative and as Secretary of State under Polk, the fifteenth President, a Democrat, came into office during the troubled years immediately preceeding the Civil War, having defeated J. C. Frémont, first candidate of the new Republican party. "They tell me," he said, "that the use of my name will still the agitated waters, restore public harmony by banishing sectionalism, and remove all apprehension for disunion. For these objects I would not only surrender my own ease and comfort, but cheerfully lay down my life." His hopes were vain. His mistakes in office have been so emphasized that his great patriotism has been overlooked.

ANDREW JOHNSON

1808–1875, PRESIDENT, 1865–1869

No other "accidental President" has ever fallen heir to heavier burdens than those which descended upon the shoulders of Andrew Johnson. He fought for the temperate reconstruction measures advocated by Lincoln, but the radicals in a Republican Congress, Charles Sumner, Thad Stevens, and Edward Stanton, blocked his efforts. Thus was fostered a bitterness between North and South for which there was no reason. He was finally impeached by the House of Representatives but, brought to trial before the Senate, he was acquitted by the narrow margin of one vote. His career as President was one long tragedy. He was in part vindicated before his death when Tennessee returned him to his old seat in the Senate.

ULYSSES SIMPSON GRANT

1822–1885, PRESIDENT, 1869–1877

His prominence as a soldier made Grant a logical candidate and he was twice elected by the Republicans. His second term was a troubled one. He found it impossible to believe that anyone could prove unworthy of his friendship, but many were just that, and his official family bred a host of political scandals. Later, in civilian life, this same simple faith led to the loss of his fortune which he retrieved by writing his charming memoirs, an act as brave as anything he ever did, for he suffered tortures from cancer of the throat during their writing and died four days after completing the manuscript. The country forgave him his shortcomings, however, and he remained a national hero to the end.

462

JAMES ABRAM GARFIELD

1831–1881, PRESIDENT, 1881

A self-made statesman, born in a log cabin in Cuyahoga County, Ohio, Garfield had an honorable record behind him when he became President. His service in the Civil War had been rewarded with the title of Major General, and his career in the House of Representatives had made him undisputed leader of the Republican party there. He was the object of violent personal abuse during the campaign, but the charges were undoubtedly false. His sound qualities promised well for his administration, but a few months after his inauguration he was fatally shot while on his way to a Commencement at Williams College by a half-crazed disappointed office seeker, Charles Guiteau.

463

RUTHERFORD BIRCHARD HAYES

1822–1893, PRESIDENT, 1877–1881

The Greenback party made its entrance into national politics in the Presidential campaign of 1876, but the real issue lay between the Republicans with Rutherford B. Hayes of Ohio and the Democrats with Samuel J. Tilden of New York. The contest was close. Under Hayes a more lenient policy was adopted toward the South; the Federal troops were withdrawn, and so ended the disgraceful "carpet-bag governments" of the post-war years. A sincere advocate of sound money, he had much to do with returning the country to prosperity after the war. Mrs. Hayes was keenly interested in public affairs and may be set down as the first modern woman in the White House.

CHESTER ALAN ARTHUR
1830–1886, PRESIDENT, 1881–1885

Although Arthur had always been deeply immersed in New York local political activities, many of an unsavory character, his term as President was notable for its honesty and dignity. His fairness and courage in the administration of the duties of his office won him the country's confidence and resulted in national unity. Lacking in dramatic events, his single term was marked by the passage of the Tariff Act of 1883. Although an advocate of the "spoils system" which was responsible for widespread corruption among government job holders, he signed the Pendleton Act of 1883, a bill providing for competitive examinations as the basis for promotion in the country's Civil Service.

(STEPHEN) GROVER CLEVELAND
1837–1908, PRESIDENT, 1885–1889, 1893–1897

Grover Cleveland was the first Democrat in twenty-three years to become President. From 1861 to his inauguration, six successive Republicans had held the office of Chief Executive. He was the first President to marry in the White House and he is the only President to serve two non-consecutive terms. Cleveland's second term was marked by the "free-silver" controversy, labor troubles (most notable of which was the famous Pullman strike at Chicago which was finally ended by the use of Federal troops), financial disturbances, and a threat of war with Great Britain over a Venezuela boundary dispute, but he conducted himself with such fairness that he won the respect even of his enemies.

464

WILLIAM McKINLEY

1843–1901, PRESIDENT, 1897–1901

Even if he had never become President, McKinley would be remembered by the protective tariff bill which bears his name. After seven terms in Congress and two terms as Governor of Ohio, he was nominated for the Presidency by the Republican party. Like Harding, he conducted his campaign from his front porch and won the election, chiefly by upholding the gold standard against the free coinage of silver advocated by the Democratic candidate, William Jennings Bryan. In 1900 approval was given his conduct of the Spanish-American War when he was renominated by acclamation. The following year on Sept. 6 at the Pan-American Exposition in Buffalo he was shot by an anarchist, Leon Czolgosz, and died on Sept. 14.

465

BENJAMIN HARRISON

1833–1901, PRESIDENT, 1889–1893

Benjamin Harrison was the grandson of the ninth President, William Henry Harrison, and the great-grandson and namesake of the Benjamin Harrison who signed the Declaration of Independence. He had fought with conspicuous gallantry in the Civil War and had settled down to law practice in Indianapolis when he was drafted for public service. Running against Cleveland, he won the election, chiefly on the issue of the protective tariff, and under him "protection" was epitomized in the McKinley Tariff Act. His administration was marked by a revival of industry and the redemption of the national debt, but the Treasury surplus became so large that Congress took occasion to enact various costly bills.

THEODORE ROOSEVELT

1858–1919, PRESIDENT, 1901–1909

Perhaps the most versatile of our Presidents was the young statesman, man of letters, sportsman, naturalist, and explorer, Theodore Roosevelt. He was the youngest man ever to assume office. Conservative by nature, he saw, however, that big business had become fat and corrupt and would ruin the country if not checked; but his fight was against corruption, not against bigness. He introduced the concept of national conservation, cleaned house in the Army, built up the Navy, sent it around the world to impress Japan, acquired land for and began the Panama Canal, and transformed the United States from adolescence to adulthood, feared, envied, but respected by all and proud of its new strength.

WILLIAM HOWARD TAFT

1857–1930, PRESIDENT, 1909–1913

When Theodore Roosevelt retired from the Presidency in 1909 he selected his Secretary of War as his successor. The Republican party acquiesced and Taft won the election by a plurality of more than a million popular votes over the Democratic nominee, William Jennings Bryan, who went down to defeat for the third and last time. Taft had not sought the office. By nature and training he was a judge, not an executive, and his ambition pointed to the Supreme Court, not the White House. This ambition was gratified in 1921 when Harding appointed him Chief Justice. He was the only man who has been both President and Chief Justice, and he filled both offices with honor to himself.

466

WARREN GAMALIEL HARDING

1865–1923, PRESIDENT, 1921–1923

With Wilson at the lowest ebb of his popularity, the country repudiated him and his party in 1920 and elected the Republican candidate. In his first message to Congress, Harding begged for a "return to normalcy," as he put it. He made earnest efforts in this direction, but his too-great confidence in certain unworthy friends whom he made Cabinet officials has caused his administration to be remembered chiefly for the scandals connected with the Teapot Dome oil cases. He died suddenly on August 2, 1923, on the way home from Alaska, before the full import of the scandals became public. In foreign affairs the high-water mark of his term was the Washington Conference for naval disarmament.

(THOMAS) WOODROW WILSON

1856–1924, PRESIDENT, 1913–1921

The twenty-eighth President was nationally known as an educator when he forsook his scholarly career to become Governor of New Jersey. Two years later the split in the Republican party (the "Bull Moose" movement) which followed the quarrel between Taft and Roosevelt made him President. In 1916 he was elected because "he kept us out of war"; but our inevitable entrance into the conflict came shortly after his second inauguration. His celebrated "fourteen points" formed the basis of the peace treaty, and he is regarded as the principal founder of the League of Nations. He was shy by nature, and when he stumped the country for the League, he failed woefully to carry the people with him.

467

CALVIN COOLIDGE

1872–1933, PRESIDENT, 1923–1929

At 2 A.M. on August 3, 1923, when word was received that President Harding had died, Vice-President Coolidge succeeded to the Presidency. The oath of office was administered in the parlor of his father's farmhouse in Plymouth, Vermont, by his father. His administration covered the boom years, but his watchfulness over the public treasury made "Coolidge economy" a by-word. Because he was "predictable" and because the country was enjoying year after year of prosperity he won a tremendous prestige with the common citizen. He was reëlected in 1924 and might have been a candidate for another term if he had not killed the movement by his famous words, "I do not choose to run for President in 1928."

HERBERT CLARK HOOVER

1874–   , PRESIDENT, 1929–1933

The thirty-first President was the first Quaker to become Chief Executive. His engineering profession had carried him all over the world, and his relief work in Belgium after the war had made him world famous. His only previous political experience had been gained as Secretary of Commerce under Harding and Coolidge. His administration was but a few months old when the stock-market crash ushered in the depression which soon became world-wide. As "bad times" deepened his prestige declined; what efforts he made to turn the tide Congress opposed, and he was defeated when he sought reëlection. His was a personality not ideally suited to politics. He continued to influence party affairs.

468

FRANKLIN DELANO ROOSEVELT

1882–   , PRESIDENT, 1933–

When he was stricken with infantile paralysis in 1921, it was believed that the political career of Franklin D. Roosevelt had come to an end, but the real mettle of this man was not then known. He had been Assistant Secretary of the Navy in World War I, Vice-Presidential candidate in 1920, and Governor of New York from 1928 until his election as President at the very nadir of the depression. His campaign for "the forgotten man" was translated into a program of wide social and economic reform known as the New Deal. It was aimed especially at financial reform, direct and indirect help for the unemployed, farm relief and conservation, better housing, and a marked tendency toward revision of the nation's whole economic structure in the interest of redistribution of the wealth. Such a liberal program naturally brought bitter opposition in some quarters but, aided by a winning personality, he again swept the country in 1936, and in 1940 became the first man elected three times to the Presidency. In his third term international affairs and World War II overshadowed events at home, and the President became the leader of that growing section of public opinion which favored more active participation in the war and in the world's affairs after it. It was generally assumed that if, on the expiration of his third term, the United States was still at war he would run again in 1944. The President's wife took a more active part in the affairs of the day than any other First Lady had ever done and herself thereby became the center of much controversy.

469